THE EGYPTIAN BOOK OF THE DEAD

THE EGYPTIAN BOOK OF THE DEAD

amber
BOOKS

This pocket illustrated edition first published in 2025 by
Amber Books Ltd
United House
North Road
London N7 9DP
United Kingdom
www.amberbooks.co.uk
Facebook: amberbooks
YouTube: amberbooksltd
Instagram: amberbooksltd
X(Twitter): @amberbooks

Copyright © 2025 Amber Books Ltd

All rights reserved. No part of this work may be reproduced, stored in a retrieval system, or transmitted in any form or by any means, electronic, mechanical, photocopying, recording, or otherwise, without the prior permission of the copyright holder.

ISBN: 978-1-83886-584-9

Printed in China

From the *Papyrus of Ani* (1240 BC)

Translated by E.A. Wallis Budge

Consultant Editor: Nigel Fletcher-Jones
Project Editors: Michael Spilling and Anna Brownbridge
Design: Mark Batley and Keren Harragan
Picture Research: Terry Forshaw

CONTENTS

INTRODUCTION *by Nigel Fletcher-Jones*   6

A HYMN OF PRAISE TO RA WHEN HE RISES

IN THE EASTERN PART OF HEAVEN   12

A HYMN TO OSIRIS UN-NEFER   17

THE JUDGEMENT OF THE DEAD   20

CHAPTERS OF COMING FORTH BY DAY   24

TEXTS RELATING TO THE WEIGHING OF THE HEART OF ANI   32

THE SEVEN ARITS   67

PYLONS OF THE HOUSE OF OSIRIS   75

THE PRIESTS ANMUTEF AND SAMEREF   81

THE JUDGES OF ANU   84

THE CHAPTER COLLECTION   94

THE SOLAR LITANY   128

THE CHAPTER OF THE NEW MOON   142

THE NEGATIVE CONFESSION   191

DIVINE UTTERANCES   206

GLOSSARY   218

INTRODUCTION

Although the term *The Egyptian Book of the Dead* is well-known today, it originated only in the 19th century when villagers digging among the cemeteries on the west bank of the Nile near Luxor in southern Egypt were heard to refer in Arabic to the papyrus sheets and scrolls they found regularly in tombs as 'dead people's books'. Making use of this, the German Egyptologist, Karl Richard Lepsius, first referred to such a text as a 'Totenbuch' (*'Book of the Dead'*) in 1842 and the name has continued to be used by Egyptologists ever since.

The Coming Forth by Day, as the ancient Egyptians called this document, is not a book as we would understand one now. There is no overarching narrative structure; for much of their history no set order was applied to the spells, hymns, and incantations; and, certainly, there was no single author. Some of the spells may even pre-date the formation of the Egyptian state around 3100 BC, and more spells were added to the collection throughout its history – even if they were based on very different mythological frameworks that had developed over many intervening centuries.

The underlying myths stretch from an ancient belief that the afterlife would be enjoyed among the circumpolar stars, to an emphasis on the supreme importance of the sun-god Ra and his associated deities – a supreme importance that was itself superseded by that of the god Osiris as judge of the dead. One of the great strengths of ancient Egyptian thought about divine matters was that it exhibited great flexibility and readily absorbed elements that we would see as contradictory or inconsistent.

The earliest written versions of some of the *Book of the Dead* spells are still to be seen in the burial chamber of King Unas (r. 2375–2345 BC) at Saqqara, southwest of modern Cairo. The use of these 'pyramid texts' was initially restricted to royalty and senior nobles, but, around 2100 BC, many more spells – increasingly written in a cursive script rather than in formal hieroglyphs – began to appear within the coffins of scribes, officials, and priests. These 'coffin texts' were the precursor of the *Book of the Dead*. All but 75 of the 192 known spells of the *Book of the Dead* are thought to be derived from the coffin texts.

The first papyrus collections of the spells appeared around 1600 BC (or slightly later), but by around 1450 BC they were fairly commonly associated with the burials of state officials. Further into the New Kingdom period (1550–1069 BC) and beyond, thousands of copies of the spells were produced by scribes, mostly on papyrus. The *Book of the Dead* was never a secret text and soon after many ancient Egyptians were buried with a copy. The best of these, like the *Papyrus of Ani*, were considerable works of art – some of the spells selected by the client being interspersed with fine illustrations ('vignettes'). The worst copies were mass-produced by scribes who simply inserted the name of the deceased. Sometimes, even this

"Homage to thee, Osiris, Lord of eternity, King of the Gods..."

seemingly vital step was left out. The practice of including a *Book of the Dead* in burials – inside the coffin or within a statue of Osiris – finally died out only in the Roman period.

The *Book of the Dead* has always been a complex document to read – ancient Egyptian scribes thought it necessary to add commentaries (marked as '*Scribes Notes*' here) to explain parts to the reader, but, nonetheless, it allows us some extraordinary insight into how ancient Egyptians thought.

Due to this partial insight, the texts have often captured the modern imagination, not least through the highly influential translation of the *Papyrus of Ani* by Sir E.A. Wallis Budge (1857–1934), which is presented in the following pages. Wallis Budge's work has a lyrical, timeless feel to it, which is emphasised here. Even without a detailed knowledge of ancient Egyptian mythology, many readers will be broadly familiar already with his description of the judgement scene in which the heart of Ani is weighed against the feather of Maat (representing truth and justice) while the god Anubis checks the balance and Thoth notes the result.

We know almost nothing about Ani himself beyond that he was a scribe in Thebes (modern Luxor) around 1250 BC – the papyrus was bought by Wallis Budge from antiquities dealers in Luxor and eventually found its way to the British Museum, where he became keeper of the Department of Egyptian and Assyrian Antiquities in 1894; but we do have some understanding of the importance of the book to its original owner.

The spells, incantations, and hymns you are about to read were intended to assist the deceased in the long, arduous, and terrifying journey through the Otherworld (as the collection also includes hymns of praise and instructions in addition to spells and incantations, some Egyptologists – like Wallis Budge – prefer to use the term 'Chapters' for the sections of the *Book of the Dead* and that has been retained below). There is some evidence within the *Book of the Dead* that the document may have been read and rehearsed by the living reader, but the spells were certainly intended to be spoken by the deceased – sometimes over a specified ritual object described in some of the scribe's annotations. A great emphasis is made throughout on the names of gods, demons, and spirits because knowing and saying the name, it was believed, gave the deceased power over them. As we shall see, during the journey the 'Osiris' (meaning the 'deceased') Ani, also became identified directly with both the sun-god Ra and the god of the dead Osiris.

The ultimate goal of Ani and his wife Tutu (who appears in some of the vignettes) was an eternity spent in the 'Field of Reeds' – an idealized form of their mortal life on the banks of the Nile, surrounded by servants to do the necessary agricultural labour, but now also protected by the gods and without the fear of the future intervention of death.

– Nigel Fletcher-Jones
(Consultant Editor)

FURTHER READING

The *Egyptian Book of the Dead* is a complex document, of which the *Papyrus of Ani* is a single, but fascinating, example and Barry Kemp's excellent *How to Read the Book of the Dead* is an invaluable source for entering further into the ancient Egyptian mindset surrounding these texts. R.O. Faulkner's *The Ancient Egyptian Book of the Dead* also elegantly details 189 spells, prayers, and incantations. Rather more detailed and encompassing a wider range of funerary texts and their history, Erik Hornung's *The Ancient Egyptian Books of the Afterlife* supplies a good overview and a wealth of bibliographic detail. In a wider context, Geraldine Pinch's *Egyptian Mythology: A Very Short Introduction* is a highly readable access point into the world view of this ancient civilization. Richard Wilkinson's *The Complete Gods and Goddesses of Ancient Egypt* forms a well-illustrated and encyclopaedic guide to the complex world of Egyptian deities. For a brief review of the history and culture of ancient Egypt, Nigel Fletcher-Jones's *Treasures of Ancient Egypt* is a concise starting point.

A HYMN OF PRAISE TO RA WHEN HE RISES IN THE EASTERN PART OF HEAVEN

Behold, Osiris Ani, the scribe who records the holy offerings of all the gods, who says: "Homage to thee, O thou who has come as Khepera, Khepera, the creator of the gods." Thou rises, thou shines, making bright thy mother [Nut], crowned king of the gods. [Thy] mother Nut pays homage unto thee with both her hands. The land of Manu receives thee with content, and the goddess Maat embraces thee at the two seasons. May he give splendour, and power, and triumph, and a coming forth as a living soul to see Horus of the two horizons to the ka of Osiris, the scribe Ani, triumphant before Osiris, who says: "Hail all ye gods of the Temple of the Soul, who weigh heaven and earth in the balance, and who provide food and abundance of meat. Hail Tatunen,

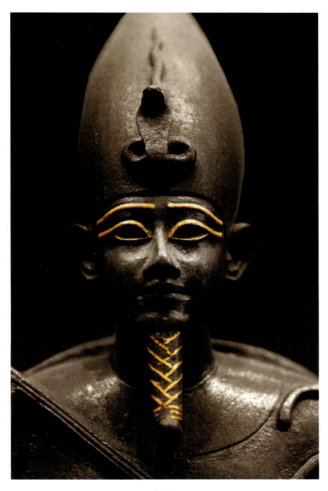

Osiris

One, creator of humankind and of the substance of the gods of the south and of the north, of the west and of the east. Ascribe [ye] praise unto Ra, the lord of heaven, the Prince, Life, Health and Strength, the Creator of the gods, and adore ye him in his beautiful Presence as he rises in the atet boat. They who dwell in the heights and they who dwell in the depths worship thee. Thoth and Maat both are thy recorders. Thine enemy is given to the fire, the evil one has fallen; his arms are bound, and Ra has taken his legs from him. The children of impotent revolt shall never rise up again."

"The House of the Prince keeps festival, and the sound of those who rejoice is in the mighty dwelling. The gods are glad [when] they see Ra in his rising; his beams flood the world with light. (The majesty of the god, who is to be feared, sets forth and comes unto the land of Manu; he makes bright the earth at his birth each day; he comes unto the place where he was yesterday. O may thou be at peace with me; may I behold thy beauties; may I advance upon the earth; may I smite the Ass;

Detail from the Book of the Dead of the vizier Neferronpet (c. 1213 BC).

may I crush the evil one; may I destroy Apep in his hour; may I see the abtu fish at the time of his creation, and the ant fish in his creation, and the ant boat in its lake. May I see Horus in charge of the rudder, with Thoth and Maat beside him; may I grasp the bows of the sektet boat, and the stern of the atet boat. May he grant unto the ka of Osiris Ani to behold the disc of the Sun and to see the Moon-god without ceasing, every day; and may my soul come forth and walk hither and thither and wheresoever it pleases. May my name be proclaimed when it is found upon the board of the table of offerings; may offerings be made unto me in my presence, even as they are made unto the followers of Horus; may there be prepared for me a seat in the boat of the Sun on the day of the going forth of the god; and may I be received into the presence of Osiris in the land of triumph!"

A HYMN TO OSIRIS UN-NEFER

"Glory be to Osiris Un-nefer, the great god within Abydos, king of eternity, lord of the everlasting, who passes through millions of years in his existence. Eldest son of the womb of Nut, engendered by Seb the Erpat, lord of the crowns of the North and South, lord of the lofty white crown. As Prince of gods and of men he has received the crook and the flail and the dignity of his divine fathers. Let thy heart that is in the mountain of Amenta be content, for thy son Horus is established upon thy throne. Thou art crowned lord of Tattu and ruler in Abtu. Through thee the world waxes green in triumph before the might of Neb-er-tcher. He leads in his train that which is and that which is not yet, in his name Ta-her-seta-nef; he tows along the earth in triumph in his name Seker.

He is exceedingly mighty and most terrible in his name Osiris. He endures for ever and ever in his name Un-nefer. Homage to thee, King of kings, Lord of lords, Prince of princes, who from the womb of Nut has possessed the world and has ruled all lands and Akert. Thy body is of gold, thy head is of azure and emerald light encircles thee. O Ani of millions of years, all-pervading with thy body and beautiful in countenance in Ta-sert. Grant thou to the ka of Osiris, the scribe Ani, splendour in heaven and might upon earth and triumph in Neter-khert; and that I may sail down to Tattu like a living soul and up to Abtu like a bennu [phoenix]; and that I may go in and come out without repulse at the pylons of the Tuat. May there be given unto me loaves of bread in the house of coolness, and offerings of food in Annu, and a homestead for ever in Sekhet-Aru with wheat and barley."

This stela depicts the royal scribe Senu adoring the god Osiris, ruler of the underworld (ca. 1390–1352 BC). Below, Senu's son, the lector priest Pawahy, is depicted twice. Once standing and pouring a libation; once kneeling and reciting the funerary prayer inscribed in front of him.

THE JUDGEMENT OF THE DEAD

Osiris, the scribe Ani, says: "My heart my mother, my heart my mother, my heart my coming into being! May there be nothing to resist me at [my] judgement; may there be no opposition to me from the Tchatcha; may there be no parting of thee from me in the presence of him who keeps the scales! Thou art my ka within my body [which] knits and strengthens my limbs. May thou come forth to the place of happiness to which I am advancing. May the Shenit not cause my name to stink, and may no lies be spoken against me in the presence of the god! Good is it for thee to hear."

Thoth, the righteous judge of the great company of the gods who are in the presence of the god Osiris, says: "Hear ye this judgement. The

A bas relief from Abydos Temple showing the Ibis-headed god Thoth offering eternal life to pharaoh Seti I.

heart of Osiris has in very truth been weighed, and his soul has stood as a witness for him; it has been found true by trial in the Great Balance."

"There has not been found any wickedness in him; he has not wasted the offerings in the temples; he has not done harm by his deeds; and he uttered no evil reports while he was upon earth."

The great company of the gods reply to Thoth dwelling in Khemennu: "That which comes forth from thy mouth has been ordained. Osiris, the scribe Ani, triumphant, is holy and righteous. He has not sinned, neither has he done evil against us. Let it not be given to the devourer Amemet to prevail over him. Meat-offerings and entrance into the presence of the god Osiris shall be granted unto him, together with a homestead for ever in Sekhet-hetepu, as unto the followers of Horus."

Horus, the son of Isis, says: "I have come unto thee, O Un-nefer, and I have brought the Osiris Ani unto thee. His heart is [found] righteous coming forth from the balance, and it has not sinned against god or goddess. Thoth has weighed it according to the decree uttered unto him by the company of the gods; and it is very true and righteous. Grant him cakes and ale; and let him enter into the presence of Osiris; and may he be like unto the followers of Horus for ever."

Behold, Osiris Ani says: "O Lord of Amentet, I am in thy presence. There is no sin in me, I have not lied wittingly, nor have I done anything whatsoever with a false heart. Grant that I may be like those favoured ones who are round about thee, and that I may be an Osiris, greatly favoured of the beautiful god and beloved of the lord of the world, the royal scribe indeed, who loves him Ani, triumphant before the god Osiris."

CHAPTERS OF COMING FORTH BY DAY

HERE BEGIN THE CHAPTERS OF COMING FORTH BY DAY, AND OF THE SONGS OF PRAISE AND GLORIFYING, AND OF COMING FORTH FROM AND GOING INTO THE GLORIOUS NETER-KHERT IN THE BEAUTIFUL AMENTA; TO BE SAID ON THE DAY OF THE BURIAL: GOING IN AFTER COMING FORTH.

Osiris Ani, Osiris the scribe Ani, says: "Homage to thee, O bull of Amentet, Thoth the king of eternity is with me. I am the great god in the boat of the Sun; I have fought for thee. I am one of the gods, those holy princes who make Osiris victorious over his enemies on the day of weighing of words. I am thy mediator, O Osiris. I am [one] of the gods born of Nut, those who slay the foes of Osiris and hold for him in

Thoth striding (332–30 BC). Thoth, the god of writing, accounting and all things intellectual, was associated with two animals: the ibis and the baboon.

bondage the fiend Sebau. I am thy mediator, O Horus. I have fought for thee, I have put to flight the enemy for thy name's sake. I am Thoth, who has made Osiris victorious over his enemies on the day of weighing of words in the great House of the mighty Ancient One in Annu. I am Tetteti, the son of Tetteti; I was conceived in Tattu, I was born in Tattu. I am with those who weep and with the women who mourn Osiris in the double land of Rechtet; and I make Osiris victorious over his enemies. Ra commanded Thoth to make Osiris victorious over his enemies; and that which was bidden for me, Thoth did. I am with Horus on the day of the clothing of Teshtesh and of the opening of the water storehouses for the purification of the god whose heart moves not, and of the unbolting of the door of concealed things in Re-stau. I am with Horus who guards the left shoulder of Osiris in Sekhem, and I go into and come out from the divine flames on the day of the destruction of the fiends in Sekhem. I am with Horus on the day of the festivals of Osiris, making the offerings on the sixth day of the festival and on the Tenat festival in Annu. I am a priest in Tattu, in the temple of Osiris on the day of casting up the earth.

Two-sided stela of pluriform Thoth (1st–2nd century AD). From left to right: assimilated with the moon god Khonsu-Harpokrates, in baboon form, and as an ibis-headed crowned figure.

I see the things that are concealed in Re-stau. I read from the book of the festival of the Soul [which is] in Tattu. I am the sem priest, and I perform his course. I am the great chief of the work on the day of the placing of

Rite of the opening of the mouth, from the tomb of Menna, Luxor.

the hennu boat of Seker upon its sledge. I have grasped the spade on

the day of digging the ground in Suten-henen. O ye who make perfected

souls enter into the Hall of Osiris, may ye cause the perfected soul of

Osiris, the scribe Ani, victorious [in the Hall of Double Truth] enter with

you into the house of Osiris. May he hear as ye hear; may he see as ye see;

may he stand as ye stand; may he sit as ye sit!"

"O ye who give bread and ale to perfected souls in the Hall of Osiris,

give ye bread and ale at the two seasons to the soul of Osiris Ani, who is

victorious before all the gods of Abtu, and who is victorious with you."

"O ye who open the way and lay open the paths to perfected souls in

the Hall of Osiris, open ye the way and lay open the paths to the soul

of Osiris, the scribe and steward of all the divine offerings, Ani [who is

triumphant] with you. May he enter in with a bold heart and may he

come forth in peace from the house of Osiris. May he not be rejected,

may he not be turned back, may he enter in [as he] pleases, may he come forth [as he] desires and may he be victorious. May his bidding be done in the house of Osiris; may he walk, and may he speak with you, and may he be a glorified soul along with you. He has not been found wanting there, and the Balance is rid of [his] trial."

CHAPTER OF GIVING A MOUTH TO OSIRIS ANI, THE SCRIBE AND TELLER OF THE HOLY OFFERINGS OF ALL THE GODS. MAY HE BE VICTORIOUS IN NETER-KHERT!

"I rise out of the egg in the hidden land. May my mouth be given unto me that I may speak with it before the great god, the lord of the underworld. (May my hand and my arm not be forced back by the holy ministers of any god. I am Osiris, the lord of the mouth of the tomb; and Osiris, the victorious scribe Ani, has a portion with him who is upon the top of the steps. According to the desire of my heart, I have come from the Pool of Fire, and I have quenched it. Homage to thee, O thou lord of brightness, thou who art at the head of the Great House, and who dwells in night and in thick darkness; I have come unto thee. I am glorious, I am pure; my arms support thee. Thy portion shall be with those who have gone before. O grant unto me my mouth that I may speak therewith; and that I may follow my heart when it passes through the fire and darkness."

SCRIBE'S NOTE:

If this writing be known [by the deceased] upon earth, and this chapter be done into writing upon [his] coffin, he shall come forth by day in all the forms of existence that he desires, and he shall enter into place and shall not be rejected. Bread and ale and meat shall be given unto Osiris, the scribe Ani, upon the altar of Osiris. He shall enter into the Fields of Aru in peace, to learn the bidding of him who dwells in Tattu; there shall wheat and barley be given unto him; there shall he flourish as he did upon earth; and he shall do whatsoever pleases him, even as [do] the gods who are in the underworld, for everlasting millions of ages, world without end.

TEXTS RELATING TO THE WEIGHING OF THE HEART OF ANI

TEXTS RELATING TO THE WEIGHING OF THE HEART OF ANI HERE BEGIN THE PRAISES AND GLORIFYINGS OF COMING OUT FROM AND GOING INTO THE GLORIOUS NETER-KHERT IN THE BEAUTIFUL AMENTA, OF COMING OUT BY DAY IN ALL THE FORMS OF EXISTENCE THAT PLEASE HIM (THE DECEASED), OF PLAYING AT DRAUGHTS AND SITTING IN THE SEH HALL AND OF COMING FORTH AS A LIVING SOUL.

Behold Osiris, the scribe Ani, after he has come to his haven [of rest]. That which has been done upon earth [by Ani] being blessed, all the words of the god Tmu come to pass. "I am the god Tmu in [my] rising; I am the only One. I came into existence in Nu. I am Ra who rose in the beginning. [He has ruled that which he made.]"

[Scribe's notes are in italics below:]

Who then is this?

It is Ra who rose for the first time in the city of Suten-henen [crowned] as a king in [his] rising. The pillars of Shu were not as yet created, when he was upon the high place of him who is in Khemennu.

"I am the great god who gave birth to himself, even Nu, [who] created his name Paut Neteru as god."

Who then is this?

It is Ra, the creator of the name[s] of his limbs, which came into being in the form of the gods in the train of Ra.

"I am he who is not driven back among the gods."

Who then is this?

It is Tmu in his disc, or (as others say), It is Ra in his rising in the eastern horizon of heaven.

"I am Yesterday; I know Tomorrow."

Who then is this?

Yesterday is Osiris, and Tomorrow is Ra, on the day when he shall destroy the enemies of Neb-er-tcher, and when he shall establish as prince and ruler his son Horus, or (as others say) on the day when we commemorate the festival of the meeting of the dead Osiris with his father Ra, and when the battle of the gods was fought in which Osiris, lord of Amentet, was the leader.

What then is this?

It is Amentet [that is to say] the creation of the souls of the gods when Osiris was leader in Set-Amentet; or (as others say) Amentet is that which Ra has given unto me; when any god comes, he arises and does battle for it.

Polychrome relief of the sun-god Ra (Temple of Hatshepsut, New Kingdom, 18th Dynasty).

Offerings of flowers being made to Ra-Horakhty (the midday manifestatation of the sun god) in a stela from the 22nd Dynasty (945–716 BC).

"I know the god who dwells therein."

Who then is this?

It is Osiris, or (as others say), Ra is his name, even Ra the self-created.

"I am the bennu bird which is in Annu, and I am the keeper of the volume of the book of things which are and of things which shall be."

Who then is this?

It is Osiris, or (as others say), It is his dead body, or (as others say), It is his filth. The things that are and the things which shall be are his dead body; or (as others say), They are eternity and everlastingness. Eternity is the day, and everlastingness is the night.

"I am the god Amsu in his coming forth; may his two plumes be set upon my head."

Who then is this?

Amsu is Horus, the avenger of his father, and his coming forth is his birth. The plumes upon his head are Isis and Nephthys when they go forth to set themselves there, even as his protectors, and they provide that which his head lacks, or (as others say), They are the two exceedingly great uraei [cobra figures] that are upon the head of their father Tmu, or (as others say), His two eyes are the two plumes.

"Osiris Ani, the scribe of all the holy offerings, rises up in his place in triumph; he comes into his city."

What then is this?

It is the horizon of his father Tmu.

"I have made an end of my shortcomings, and I have put away my faults."

What then is this?

It is the cutting off of the corruptible in the body of Osiris, the scribe

Ani, triumphant before all the gods; and all his faults are driven out.

What then is this?

It is the purification [of Osiris] on the day of his birth.

"I am purified in my exceedingly great double nest that is in Sutenhenen, on the day of the offerings of the followers of the great god who is therein."

What then is this?

'Millions of years' is the name of the one [nest], 'Green Lake' is the name of the other; a pool of natron, and a pool of nitre; or (as others say), 'The Traverser of Millions of Years' is the name of the one, 'Great Green Lake' is the name of the other; or (as others say), 'The Begetter of Millions of Years' is the name of the one, 'Green Lake' is the name of the other. Now as concerning the great god who is in it, it is Ra himself.

"I pass over the way, I know the head of the Pool of Maata."

What then is this?

It is Re-stau; that is to say, it is the underworld on the south of Naarut-f, and it is the northern door of the tomb. Now as concerning She-Maat, it is Abtu; or (as others say), It is the road by which his father Tmu travels when he goes to Sekhet-Aru, which brings forth the food and nourishment of the gods behind the shrine. (Now the Gate of Sert is the gate of the pillars of Shu, the northern gate of the underworld; or (as others say), It is the two leaves of the door through which the god Tmu passes when he goes forth in the eastern horizon of heaven. "O ye gods who are in the presence (of Osiris), grant me your arms, for I am the god who shall come into being among you."

What then is this?

It is the drops of blood that fell from Ra when he went forth to cut himself. They sprang into being as the gods Hu and Sa, who are in the following of Ra and who accompany Tmu daily and every day.

'The Fumigation of Osiris', the Book of the Dead of Neb-Qued (19th Dynasty).

Seti I opens the door for Osiris (from the temple of King Seti I at Abydos).

"I, Osiris, Ani the scribe, triumphant, have filled up for thee the utchat after it was darkened on the day of the combat of the Two Fighters."

What then is this?

It is the day on which Horus fought with Set, who cast filth in the face of Horus, and when Horus destroyed the powers of Set. Thoth did this with his own hand.

"I lift the hair[-cloud] when there are storms in the sky."

What then is this?

It is the right eye of Ra that raged against [Set] when he sent it forth. Thoth raises up the hair[-cloud], and brings the eye alive, and whole, and sound, and without defect to [its] lord; or (as others say), It is the eye of Ra when it is sick and when it weeps for its fellow eye; then Thoth stands up to cleanse it.

"I behold Ra who was born yesterday from the buttocks of the cow Mehurt; his strength is my strength, and my strength is his strength."

What then is this?
It is the water of heaven, or (as others say), It is the image of the eye of Ra in the morning at his daily birth. Mehurt is the eye of Ra. Therefore Osiris, the scribe Ani, triumphant, [is] a great one among the gods who are in the train of Horus. The words [are] spoken for him that loves his lord.

What then is this? [who are these gods?]
Mestha, Hapi, Tuamautef and Qebhsennuf.

"Homage to you, O ye lords of right and truth, and ye holy ones who [stand] behind Osiris, who utterly do away with sins and crime, and [ye] who are in the following of the goddess Hetep-se-khus, grant that I may come unto you. Destroy ye all the faults that are within me, even as

Rare depiction of the hawk-headed god Horus smiting the god Seth, represented as a donkey (from the Ptolemaic temple of Opet, Karnak Temple).

ye did for the seven Shining Ones who are among the followers of their lord Sepa. Anubis appointed their place on the day [when was said], 'Come therefore thither.'"

What then is this?

These lords of right and truth are Thoth and Astes, lords of Amenta. The holy ones who stand behind Osiris, even Mestha, Hapi, Tuamautef and Qebhsennuf, are they who are behind the Thigh in the northern sky. They who do away with sins and crime and who are in the following of the goddess Hetep-se-khus are the god Sebek in the waters. The goddess Hetep-se-khus is the eye of Ra, or (as others say), It is the flame that follows after Osiris to burn up the souls of his foes. As concerning all the faults that are in Osiris, the scribe of the holy offerings of all the gods, Ani, triumphant [they are all that he has done against the lords of eternity] since he came forth from his mother's womb. As concerning the seven Shining Ones, even Mestha, Hapi, Tuamautef, Qebhsennuf, Maa-atef-f, Kheri-beq-f and Horus-Khenti-maa, Anubis appointed them protectors of the body of Osiris, or (as others say), [set them] behind the place of purification of Osiris; or (as others say), Those seven glorious ones are Netcheh-netcheh, Aqet-qet, An-erta-nef-bes-f-khenti-heh-f, Aq-her-unnut-f, Tesher-maa-ammi-het-Anes, Ubes-hra-per-em-khet khet and Maa-em-qerh-an-nef-em-hru. The chief of the holy ones who minister in his chamber is Horus, the avenger of his father. As to the day [upon which was said] "Come therefore thither," it concerns the words, "Come then thither," which Ra spoke unto Osiris. Lo, may this be decreed for me in Amentet.

"I am the soul that dwells in the two tchafi."

What then is this?

It is Osiris [when] he goes into Tattu and finds there the soul of Ra; there the one god embraces the other, and souls spring into being within the two tchafi.

"I am the Cat that fought hard by the persea tree in Annu, on the night when the foes of Neb-er-tcher were destroyed."

What then is this?
The male cat is Ra himself, and he is called Maau by reason of the speech of the god Sa [who said] concerning him: "He is like (maau) unto that which he has made, and his name became Maau"; or (as others say), It is Shu who makes over the possessions of Seb to Osiris. As to the fight by the persea tree in Annu, it concerns the children of impotent revolt when justice is wrought on them for what they have done. As to [the words] "that night of the battle," they concern the inroad [of the children of impotent revolt] into the eastern part of heaven, whereupon there arose a battle in heaven and in all the earth.

"O thou who art in the egg (Ra), who shines from thy disc and rises in thy horizon, and shines like gold above the sky, like unto whom there is none among the gods, who sails over the pillars of Shu (the ether), who

Stela of Aafenmut (ca. 924–889 BC). The small wooden stela is topped by the solar barque in the sky, which is supported by the emblems of the east (on the right) and the west (on the left). Aafenmut, identified here as a Scribe of the Treasury, offers incense to the seated sun god, Ra-Horakhty, who is shown as a mummy with the head of a falcon.

A detail from the Papyrus of Pajuheru shows the adoration of Osiris (Ptolemaic period, 2nd century BC).

gives blasts of fire from thy mouth, [who makes the two lands bright with thy radiance, deliver] the faithful worshippers from the god whose forms are hidden, whose eyebrows are like unto the two arms of the balance on the night of the reckoning of destruction."

Who then is this?
It is An-a-f, the god who brings his arm. As concerning [the words] "that night of the reckoning of destruction," it is the night of the burning of the damned, and of the overthrow of the wicked at [the sacred] block, and of the slaughter of souls.

Who then is this?
It is Nemu, the headsman of Osiris; or (as others say), It is Apep when he rises up with one head bearing maat (right and truth) [upon it]; or (as others say), It is Horus when he rises up with two heads, where one bears maat and the other wickedness. He bestows wickedness on him that works wickedness, and maat on him that follows righteousness and

truth; or (as others say), It is the great Horus who dwells in [Se]khem; or (as others say), It is Thoth; or (as others say), It is Nefer-Tmu, [or] Sept, who thwarts the course of the foes of Neb-er-tcher.

"Deliver me from the watchers who bear slaughtering knives, and who have cruel fingers, and who slay those who are in the following of Osiris. May they never overcome me, may I never fall under their knives."

What then is this?
It is Anubis, and it is Horus in the form of Khent-en-maa; or, It is the Divine Rulers who thwart the works of their [weapons]; it is the chiefs of the sheniu chamber.

"May their knives never get the mastery over me, may I never fall under their instruments of cruelty, for I know their names, and I know the being Matche, who is among them in the house of Osiris, shooting

In his cat form the sun-god Ra kills the snake god Apophis, god of the underworld, shown coiled around the sacred sycamore tree (from the tomb of Inherkha, Deir el Medina, West Thebes, 20th Dynasty).

A rare wooden amulet shows the god Horus standing on two captives' heads (664–30 BC).

rays of light from [his] eye, but he himself is unseen. He goes round about heaven robed in the flame of his mouth, commanding Hapi, but remaining himself unseen. May I be strong upon earth before Ra, may I come happily into haven in the presence of Osiris. Let not your offerings be hurtful to me, O ye who preside over your altars, for I am among those who follow after Neb-er-tcher according to the writings of Khepera. I fly as a hawk, I cackle as a goose; I ever slay, even as the serpent goddess Nehebka."

What then is this?
They who preside at the altars are the similitude of the eye of Ra and the similitude of the eye of Horus.

"O Ra-Tmu, lord of the Great House, prince, life, strength and health of all the gods, deliver thou [me] from the god whose face is like that of a dog, whose brows are as those of a man, and who feeds upon the dead, who watches at the Bight of the Fiery Lake, and who devours the bodies of the dead and swallows hearts, and who shoots forth filth, but he himself remains unseen."

Who then is this?

'Devourer for millions of years' is his name, and he dwells in the Lake of Unt. As concerning the Fiery Lake, it is that which is in Anrutf, hard by the Shenit chamber. The unclean man who would walk there falls down among the knives; or (as others say), His name is 'Mathes,' and he is the watcher of the door of Amenta; or (as others say), His name is 'Heri-sep-f.'

"Hail, Lord of terror, chief of the lands of the North and South, lord of the red glow, who prepares the slaughter-block, and who feeds upon the inward parts!"

Who then is this?

The guardian of the shore of Amenta.

A Greco-Roman stela of two snake goddesses (Egyptian Museum).

Detail of an Egyptian papyrus showing the protective eye of Horus.

What then is this?

It is the heart of Osiris, which is the devourer of all slaughtered things.

The urerit crown has been given unto him with swellings of the heart as lord of Suten-henen.

What then is this?

He to whom has been given the urerit crown with swellings of the heart as lord of Suten-henen is Osiris. He was bidden to rule among the gods on the day of the union of earth with earth in the presence of Neb-er-tcher.

What then is this?
He that was bidden to rule among the gods is [Horus] the son of Isis, who was appointed to rule in the place of his father Osiris. As to the day of the union of earth with earth, it is the mingling of earth with earth in the coffin of Osiris, the Soul that lives in Suten-henen, the giver of meat and drink, the destroyer of wrong and the guide of the everlasting paths.

Who then is this?
It is Ra himself.

"Deliver thou [me] from the great god who carries away souls, and who devours filth and eats dirt, the guardian of the darkness [who himself lives] in the light. They who are in misery fear him."

As concerning the souls within the tchafi [they are those that are] with the god who carries away the soul, who eats hearts and who feeds upon offal, the guardian of the darkness who is within the seker boat; they who live in crime fear him.

Who then is this?
It is Suti, or (as others say), it is Smam-ur, the soul of Seb.

"Hail, Khepera in thy boat, the two-fold company of the gods is thy body. Deliver thou Osiris Ani, triumphant, from the watchers who give judgement, who have been appointed by Neb-er-tcher to protect him and to fasten the fetters on his foes, and who slaughter in the shambles; there is no escape from their grasp. May they never stab me with their knives, may I never fall helpless in their chambers of torture.

Ramesses' queen, Sitre, shakes two sistra, which were associated with the god Hathor (relief from the South Wall of a Chapel of Ramesses I, ca. 1295–1294 BC).

Never have the things that the gods hate been done by me, for I am pure within the Mesqet. Cakes of saffron have been brought unto him in Tanenet."

Who then is this?

It is Khepera in his boat. It is Ra himself. The watchers who give

The Barge of Khepri (depicted with a scarab beetle head), the Egyptian solar deity (from a 21st Dynasty funerary papyrus).

judgement are the apes Isis and Nephthys. The things that the gods hate are wickedness and falsehood; and he who passes through the place of purification within the Mesqet is Anubis, who is behind the chest that holds the inward parts of Osiris.

He to whom saffron cakes have been brought in Tanenet is Osiris; or (as others say), The saffron cakes in Tanenet are heaven and earth, or (as others say), They are Shu, strengthener of the two lands in Sutenhenen. The saffron cakes are the eye of Horus; and Tanenet is the grave of Osiris.

Tmu has built thy house, and the two-fold Lion-god has founded thy habitation; lo! drugs are brought, and Horus purifies and Set strengthens, and Set purifies and Horus strengthens.

"The Osiris, the scribe Ani, triumphant before Osiris, has come into the land, and has possessed it with his feet. He is Tmu, and he is in the city."

"Turn thou back, O Rehu, whose mouth shines, whose head moves, turn thou back from before his strength"; or (as others say), Turn thou back from him who keeps watch and is unseen. "The Osiris Ani is safely guarded. He is Isis, and he is found with [her] hair spread over him. I shake it out over his brow. He was conceived in Isis and begotten in Nephthys; and they cut off from him the things that should be cut off."

Fear follows after thee, terror is upon thine arms. Thou art embraced for millions of years in the arms [of the nations]; mortals go round about thee. Thou smites down the mediators of thy foes, and thou seizes the arms of the powers of darkness. The two sisters (Isis and Nephthys) are given to thee for thy delight. Thou has created that which is in Kheraba, and that which is in Annu. Every god fears thee, for thou art exceedingly great and terrible; thou [avenges] every god on the man that curses him, and thou shoots out arrows… Thou lives according to thy will; thou art Uatchit, the Lady of Flame. Evil comes among those who set themselves up against thee.

What then is this?

The hidden in form, granted of Menhu, is the name of the tomb. He sees [what is] in [his] hand is the name of the shrine, or (as others say), the name of the block. Now he whose mouth shines and whose head moves is a limb of Osiris, or (as others say), of Ra. "Thou spreads thy hair and I shake it out over his brow" is spoken concerning Isis, who hides in her hair and draws her hair over her. Uatchi, the Lady of Flame, is the eye of Ra.

Bronze figure of the goddess Wadjet with the head of a lioness. She is most often represented by a striking cobra's head, as can be seen on her crown here.

THE SEVEN ARITS

THE FIRST ARIT [Gate]

The name of the doorkeeper is Sekhet-hra-asht-aru; the name of the watcher is Meti-heh; the name of the herald is Ha-kheru.

Words to be spoken when Osiris comes to the first Arit in Amenta: Says Ani, triumphant, when he comes to the first Arit: "I am the mighty one who creates his own light. I have come unto thee, O Osiris, and, purified from that which defiles thee, I adore thee. Lead on; name not the name of Re-stau unto me. Homage to thee, O Osiris, in thy might and in thy strength in Re-stau. Rise up and conquer, O Osiris, in Abtu. Thou goes round about heaven, thou sails in the presence of Ra, thou sees all the beings who have knowledge. Hail Ra, who circles in [the sky]. Verily I say [unto thee], O Osiris, I am a godlike ruler. Let me not be driven hence nor from the wall of burning coals. [I have] opened the way in Re-stau; I have eased the pain of Osiris; [I have] embraced that which the balance I have weighed; [I have] made a path for him in the great valley, it and [he] make a path. Osiris shines."

THE SECOND ARIT

The name of the doorkeeper is Un-hat; the name of the watcher is Seqet-hra; the name of the herald is Uset.

Says Osiris Ani, when he comes unto this Arit; "He sits to do his heart's desire, and he weighs words as the second of Thoth. The strength of Thoth humbles the hidden Maata gods who feed upon Maat throughout the years [of their lives]. I make offerings at the moment when [he] passes on his way; I pass on and enter on the way; Grant thou that I may pass through and that I may gain sight of Ra together with those who make offerings."

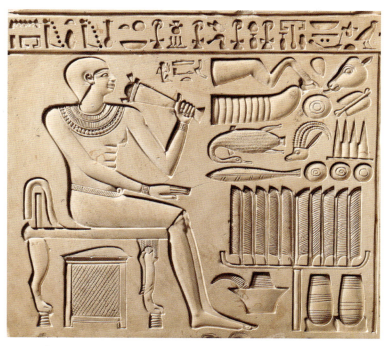

The minor official Maati seated in front of an offering table (c. 2051–2030 BC)

Part of a funerary papyrus (ca. 230–150 BC) showing the judgment before Osiris. This fragment depicts the ritual of the Weighing of the Heart, in which the deceased demonstrated that he or she had lived an ethical life. This trial took place in the Netherworld, in the Hall of the Two Truths. The architecture of this chamber is defined by two papyrus columns topped by a cavetto cornice. The top of the cornice is protected by alternating ostrich plumes, the hieroglyphs for maat, or truth, braziers representing fire, and rearing cobras.

THE THIRD ARIT

The name of the doorkeeper is Qeq-hauau-ent-pehui; the name of the watcher is Se-res-hra; the name of the herald is Aaa.

Says Osiris Ani, [when he comes to this Arit]: "I am hidden [in] the great deep, [I am] the judge of the Rehui. I have come and I have done away with the offences of Osiris. I am building up the standing place that comes forth from his urerit crown. I have done his business in Abtu, I have opened the way in Re-stau, I have eased the pain that was in Osiris. I have made straight his standing place, and I have made [his] path. He shines in Re-stau."

THE FOURTH ARIT

The name of the doorkeeper is Khesef-hra-asht-kheru; the name of the watcher is Seres-tepu; the name of the herald is Khesef-At.

Says Osiris, the scribe Ani, triumphant, [when he comes to this Arit]:

"I am the [mighty] bull, the son of the ancestress of Osiris. O grant ye that his father, the lord of his godlike companions, may bear witness for him. Here the guilty are weighed in judgement. I have brought unto his nostrils eternal life. I am the son of Osiris, I have made the way, I have passed thereover into Neter-khert."

THE FIFTH ARIT

The name of the doorkeeper is Ankh-f-em-fent; the name of the watcher is Shabu; the name of the herald is Teb-hra-keha-kheft.

Says Osiris, the scribe Ani, triumphant, [when he comes to this Arit]:
I have brought unto thee the bones of thy jaws in Re-stau, I have brought thee thy backbone in Annu, gathering together all thy members there. I have driven back Apep for thee. I have poured water upon the wounds; I have made a path among you. I am the Ancient One among the gods. I have made the offering of Osiris, who has triumphed with victory, gathering his bones and bringing together all his limbs."

Book of the Dead for the chantress of Amun, Nauny (ca. 1050 BC). The heart of the deceased (left) is weighed against a statue of the goddess Maat, representing truth and cosmic order.

THE SIXTH ARIT

The name of the doorkeeper is Atek-au- kehaq-kheru; the name of the watcher is An-hri; the name of the herald is Ates-hra.

Says Osiris, the scribe Ani, [when he comes to this Arit]: "I have come daily, I have come daily. I have made the way; I have passed along that which was created by Anubis. I am the lord of the urerit crown …

magical words. I, the avenger of right and truth, have avenged his eye. I have swathed the eye of Osiris, [I have] made the way; Osiris Ani has passed along [it] with you…"

THE SEVENTH ARIT

The name of the doorkeeper is Sekhem-Matenu-sen; the name of the watcher is Aa-maa-kheru; the name of the herald is Khesef-khemi.

Says Osiris, [the scribe] Ani, [when he comes to this Arit]: "I have come unto thee, O Osiris, who art cleansed of [thine] impurities. Thou goes round about heaven, thou sees Ra, thou sees the beings who have knowledge. Hail Only One! behold, thou art in the sektet boat, He goes round the horizon of heaven. I speak what I will unto his body; it waxes strong and it comes to life, as he spoke. Thou turns back his face. Prosper thou for me all the ways [that lead] unto thee!"

PYLONS OF THE HOUSE OF OSIRIS

WORDS TO BE SPOKEN WHEN [ANI] COMES UNTO THE FIRST PYLON

Says Osiris Ani, triumphant: "Lo, the lady of terrors, with lofty walls, the sovereign lady, the mistress of destruction, who utters the words that drive back the destroyers, who delivers from destruction him that travels along the way. The name of the doorkeeper is Neruit."

WORDS TO BE SPOKEN WHEN [ANI] COMES UNTO THE SECOND PYLON

Says Osiris, the scribe Ani, triumphant: "Lo, the lady of heaven, the mistress of the world, who devours with fire, the lady of mortals; how much greater is she than all men! The name of the doorkeeper is Mes-Ptah."

WORDS TO BE SPOKEN WHEN [ANI] COMES UNTO THE THIRD PYLON OF THE HOUSE OF OSIRIS

Says the scribe Ani, triumphant: "Lo, the lady of the altar, the mighty one to whom offerings are made, the beloved of every god, who sails up to Abtu. The name of the doorkeeper is Sebaq."

WORDS TO BE SPOKEN WHEN [ANI] COMES UNTO THE FOURTH PYLON

Says Osiris, the scribe Ani, [triumphant]: "Lo, she who prevails with knives, mistress of the world, destroyer of the foes of the Still-Heart, she who decrees the escape of the needy from evil hap (fortune). The name of the doorkeeper is Nekau."

WORDS TO BE SPOKEN WHEN [ANI] COMES UNTO THE FIFTH PYLON

Says Osiris, the scribe Ani, triumphant: "Lo, the flame, the lady of breath for the nostrils; one may not advance to entreat her, shall not

A detail from the Papyrus of Ani (sheet 4), showing the conclusion of the judgement, with Ani introduced to Osiris.

Ani and his wife approach the Seven Gates of Arit (from the 10 pylons of Osiris). Some of the seven gates (Arits) are above. Some of the 10 pylons are below.

come into her presence. The name of the doorkeeper is Hentet-Arqiu."

WORDS TO BE SPOKEN WHEN [ANI] COMES UNTO THE SIXTH PYLON

Says Osiris, the scribe Ani, triumphant: "Lo, the lady of light, the mighty one, to whom men cry aloud; man knows neither her breadth nor her height; there was never found her like from the beginning.

There is a serpent thereover whose size is not known; it was born in the presence of the Still-Heart. The name of the doorkeeper is Semati."

WORDS TO BE SPOKEN WHEN [ANI] COMES UNTO THE SEVENTH PYLON

Says Osiris, the scribe Ani, triumphant: "Lo, the robe that clothes the feeble one (the deceased), weeping for what it loves and shrouds. The name of the doorkeeper is Sakti-f."

WORDS TO BE SPOKEN WHEN [ANI] COMES UNTO THE EIGHTH PYLON

Says Osiris, the scribe Ani, triumphant: "Lo, the blazing fire, the flame whereof cannot be quenched, with tongues of flame that reach afar, the slaughtering one, the irresistible, through which one may not pass by reason of the hurt that it does. The name of the doorkeeper is Khu-tchet-f."

WORDS TO BE SPOKEN WHEN [ANI] COMES UNTO THE NINTH PYLON

Says Osiris Ani, triumphant: "Lo, she who is chiefest, the lady of strength, who gives quiet of heart to her lord. Her girth is three hundred and fifty measures; she is clothed with mother-of-emerald of the south; and she raises up the godlike form and clothes the feeble one. The name of the doorkeeper is Ari-su-tchesef."

WORDS TO BE SPOKEN WHEN [ANI] COMES UNTO THE TENTH PYLON

Says Osiris Ani, [triumphant]: "Lo, she who is loud of voice, she who causes those to cry who entreat her, the fearful one who terrifies, who fears none that are therein. The name of the doorkeeper is Sekhen-ur."

THE PRIESTS ANMUTEF AND SAMEREF

[The Priest] Anmutef says: "I have come unto you, O mighty and godlike rulers who are in heaven and in earth and under the earth; and I have brought unto you Osiris Ani. He has not sinned against any of the gods. Grant ye that he may be with you for all time."

The adoration of Osiris, lord of Re-stau, and of the great company of the gods who are in the netherworld beside Osiris, the scribe Ani, who says: "Homage to thee, O ruler of Amenta, Un-nefer within Abtu! I have come unto thee, and my heart holds right and truth. There is no sin in my body; nor have I lied wilfully, nor have I done anything whatsoever with a false heart. Grant thou to me food in the tomb, and that I may come into [thy] presence at the altar of the lords of right and truth, and that I may enter into and come forth from the netherworld (my soul not being turned back), and that I may behold the face of the Sun, and that I may behold the Moon for ever and ever."

[The priest] Sameref says I have come unto you, O godlike rulers who are in Re-stau, and I have brought unto you Osiris Ani. Grant ye [to him], as to the followers of Horus, cakes and water, and air, and a homestead in Sekht-hetepu." The adoration of Osiris, the lord of everlastingness, and of all the godlike rulers of Re-stau, by Osiris, [the scribe Ani], who says: "Homage to thee, O king of Amenta, prince of Akert, I have come unto thee. I know thy ways, I am furnished with the forms that thou takes in the underworld. Grant thou to me a place in the underworld near unto the lords of right and truth. May my homestead be abiding in Sekhet-hetep, and may I receive cakes in thy presence."

The daily journey of the sun-god Ra: surrounded by worshipping baboons at dawn (bottom panel); at midday (middle panel); and preparing for the nighttime journey through the Other World (top panel).

THE JUDGES OF ANNU

"Hail Thoth, who made Osiris victorious over his enemies, make thou Osiris [the scribe Ani] be victorious over his enemies, as thou did make Osiris victorious over his enemies in the presence of the godlike rulers who are with Ra and Osiris in Annu, on the night of 'the things for the night,' and on the night of battle, and on the shackling of the fiends, and on the day of the destruction of Neb-er-tcher."

The great godlike rulers in Annu are Tmu, Shu, Tefnut [Osiris and Thoth], and the shackling of the Sebau signifies the destruction of the fiends of Set when he works evil a second time.

"Hail, Thoth, who made Osiris victorious over his enemies, make thou the Osiris Ani victorious over his enemies in the presence of the great divine beings who are in Tattu, on the night of making the Tat to stand up in Tattu."

The great godlike rulers in Tattu are Osiris, Isis, Nephthys and Horus, the avenger of his father. Now the "night of making the Tat to stand up in Tattu" signifies [the lifting up of] the arm and shoulder of Osiris, lord of Sekhem; and these gods stand behind Osiris [to protect him] even as the swathings that clothe him.

"Hail, Thoth, who made Osiris victorious over his enemies, make thou the Osiris Ani triumphant over his enemies in the presence of the great godlike rulers who are in Sekhem, on the night of the things of the night [festival] in Sekhem."

The great godlike rulers who are in Sekhem are Horus, who is without sight, and Thoth, who is with the godlike rulers in Naarut-f. Now the "night of the things of the night festival in Sekhem" signifies the light of the rising sun on the coffin of Osiris.

"Hail, Thoth, who made Osiris victorious over his enemies, make thou the Osiris Ani triumphant over his enemies in the presence of the great godlike rulers in Pe and Tep, on the night of setting up the columns

Ramesses II is purified by the gods Thoth (left) and Horus (right) (from the Temple of Seti I, Abydos).

of Horus, and of making him be established the heir of the things that belonged to his father."

The great divine rulers who are in Pe and Tep are Horus, Isis, Mestha and Hapi. Now setting up the columns of Horus [signifies] the command given by Set unto his followers: "Set up columns upon it."

"Hail, Thoth, who made Osiris victorious over his enemies, make thou the Osiris-Ani triumphant over his enemies in the presence of the great godlike rulers in ... Rekhit, on the night when Isis lay down to keep watch in order to make lamentation for her brother Osiris."

The great godlike rulers who are in ... Rekhit are Isis, Horus and Mestha.

"Hail, Thoth, who made Osiris victorious over his enemies, make thou the Osiris, the scribe Ani (triumphant in peace!), be victorious over his

Offering table of Tjaenhesret, priest of Thoth, son of Iaa (332–30 BC)

enemies in the presence of the great godlike ones who are in Abtu, on the night of the god Naker, at the separation of the wicked dead, at the judgement of spirits made just, and at the arising of joy in Tenu."

The great godlike rulers who are in Abtu are Osiris, Isis and Ap-uat.

"Hail, Thoth, who made Osiris victorious over his enemies, make thou the Osiris Ani, the scribe and teller of the sacred offerings of all the gods, victorious over his enemies in the presence of the godlike rulers who judge the dead, on the night of the condemnation of those who are to be blotted out."

The great godlike rulers in the judgement of the dead are Thoth, Osiris, Anubis and Astennu. Now the "condemnation of those who are to be blotted out" is the withholding of that which is so needful to the souls of the children of impotent revolt.

"Hail, Thoth, who made Osiris victorious over his enemies, make thou the Osiris, the scribe Ani (triumphant!), victorious over his enemies in the presence of the great godlike rulers, on the festival of the breaking and turning up of the earth in Tattu, on the night of the breaking and turning up of the earth in their blood and of making Osiris be victorious over his enemies."

When the fiends of Set come and change themselves into beasts, the great godlike rulers, on the festival of the breaking and turning up of the earth in Tattu, slay them in the presence of the gods therein, and their blood flows among them as they are smitten down. These things are allowed to be done by them by the judgement of those who are in Tattu.

"Hail, Thoth, who made Osiris victorious over his enemies, make thou the Osiris Ani victorious over his enemies in the presence of the godlike rulers who are in Naarutef, on the night of him who conceals himself in diverse forms, even Osiris."

The great godlike rulers who are in Naarutef are Ra, Osiris, Shu and Bebi. Now the night of him who conceals himself in diverse forms, even Osiris, is when the thigh [and the head], and the heel, and the leg, are brought nigh unto the coffin of Osiris Un-nefer.

"Hail, Thoth, who made Osiris victorious over his enemies, make thou

The demon Amemet (Ammit), part crocodile, part lion, and part hippopotamus waits to devour the hearts of the wicked (detail from the Book of the Dead of Nebqed, 18th Dynasty, ca. 1400 BC).

the Osiris Ani (triumphant before Osiris) victorious over his enemies in the presence of the great godlike rulers who are in Restau, on the night when Anubis lay with his arms and his hands over the things behind Osiris, and when Horus was made to triumph over his enemies."

The great godlike rulers in Re-stau are Horus, Osiris and Isis. The heart of Osiris rejoices, and the heart of Horus is glad; and therefore are the east and the west at peace.

Stele of Nesptah (664–525 BC). A winged sun disk with pendant uraei *(cobras) arches across the top of this funerary stele. The central scene depicts the deceased (at the right) being ushered by Thoth into the presence of the funerary gods. Led by Osiris and Ra-Horakhty, these gods are Isis, Nephthys and the Four Sons of Horus. The tiny squares above them were intended for brief inscriptions naming each god, but the names were omitted.*

"Hail Thoth, who made Osiris victorious over his enemies, make thou the Osiris Ani, the scribe and teller of the divine offerings of all the gods, triumph over his enemies in the presence of the ten companies of great godlike rulers who are with Ra and with Osiris and with every god and goddess in the presence of Neb-er-tcher. He has destroyed his enemies, and he has destroyed every evil thing belonging unto him."

Scribe's note:

This chapter being recited, the deceased shall come forth by day, purified after death, and [he shall make all] the forms (or transformations) that his heart shall dictate. Now if this chapter be recited over him, he shall come forth upon earth, he shall escape from every fire; and none of the foul things that belong unto him shall encompass him for everlasting and for ever and for ever.

THE CHAPTER COLLECTION

THE CHAPTER OF OPENING THE MOUTH OF OSIRIS, THE SCRIBE ANI

To be said: "May Ptah open my mouth, and may the god of my town loose the swathings, even the swathings that are over my mouth. Moreover, may Thoth, being filled and furnished with charms, come and loose the bandages, the bandages of Set that fetter my mouth; and may the god Tmu hurl them at those who would fetter [me] with them, and drive them back. May my mouth be opened, may my mouth be unclosed by Shu with his iron knife, wherewith he opened the mouth of the gods. I am Sekhet, and I sit upon the great western side of heaven. I am the great goddess Sa among the souls of Annu. Now as concerning every charm and all the words that may be spoken against me, may the gods resist them, and may each and every one of the company of the gods withstand them."

THE CHAPTER OF BRINGING CHARMS UNTO OSIRIS ANI [IN NETER-KHERT]

[He says]: "I am Tmu-Khepera, who gave birth unto himself upon the thigh of his divine mother. Those who are in Nu are made wolves, and those who are among the godlike rulers are become hyenas. Behold, I gather together the charm from every place where it is and from every man with whom it is, swifter than greyhounds and fleeter than light. Hail thou who tows along the makhent boat of Ra, the stays of thy sails and of thy rudder are taut in the wind as thou sails over the Lake of Fire in Neter-khert. Behold, thou gathers together the charm from every place where it is and from every man with whom it is, swifter than greyhounds and fleeter than light, [the charm] that creates the forms of existence from the mother's thigh and creates the gods from (or in) silence, and that gives the heat of life unto the gods. Behold, the charm

Side panel from the coffin of Amenemope (ca. 976–889 BC) showing the opening of the mouth ritual.

96

is given unto me from wheresoever it is [and from him with whom it is], swifter than greyhounds and fleeter than light," or, (as others say), "fleeter than a shadow."

THE CHAPTER OF GIVING A HEART UNTO OSIRIS ANI IN THE UNDERWORLD

[Ani says]: "May my heart be with me in the House of Hearts. May my heart be with me, and may it rest in [me], or I shall not eat of the cakes of Osiris on the eastern side of the Lake of Flowers, [neither shall I have] a boat wherein to go down the Nile, and another wherein to go up, nor shall I go forward in the boat with thee. May my mouth be given unto me that I may speak with it, and my two feet to walk, and my two hands and arms to overthrow my foe. May the doors of heaven be opened unto me; may Seb, the Prince of the gods, open wide his two jaws unto me; may he open my two eyes that are blinded; may he cause me to stretch out my feet that are bound together; and may Anubis make my legs firm that I may stand upon them. May the goddess Sekhet make me rise so that I may ascend unto heaven, and there may that be done which I command in the House of the Ka of Ptah. I know my heart, I have mastery over my heart, I have mastery over my two hands and arms, I have mastery over my feet and I have gained the power to do whatsoever my ka pleases. My soul shall not be shut off from my body at the gates of the underworld; but I shall enter in peace, and I shall come forth in peace."

THE CHAPTER OF NOT LETTING THE HEART OF OSIRIS, THE SCRIBE OF THE SACRED OFFERINGS OF ALL THE GODS, ANI, TRIUMPHANT, BE DRIVEN FROM HIM IN THE UNDERWORLD

Ani says: "My heart, my mother; my heart, my mother. My heart whereby I come into being. May there be nothing to withstand me at [my] judgement; may there be no resistance against me by the Tchatcha; may there be no parting of thee from me in the presence of him who keeps the scales! Thou art my ka within my body, [which] knits and strengthens my limbs. May thou come forth in the place of

Heart Amulet (ca. 1295–1070 BC), New Kingdom period.

The god of mummification Anubis is shown here as a human with a jackal head (332–30 BC).

happiness [to which] I advance. May the Shenit, who make men stand fast, not cause my name to stink."

CHAPTER OF NOT LETTING THE SOUL OF A MAN BE TAKEN AWAY FROM HIM IN THE UNDERWORLD

Osiris the scribe Ani says: "I, even I, am he who came forth from the waterflood that I make to overflow and that becomes mighty as the River [Nile]."

CHAPTER OF GIVING BREATH IN THE UNDERWORLD

Says Osiris Ani: "I am the Egg of the Great Cackler, and I watch and guard that great place, which the god Seb has proclaimed upon earth. I live; and it lives; I grow strong, I live, I sniff the air. I am Utcha-aab, and I go round behind [to protect] his egg. I have thwarted the chance of Set, the mighty one of strength. Hail thou who makes pleasant the world with tchefa food, and who dwells in the blue [sky]; watch over the babe in his cot when he comes forth unto thee."

THE CHAPTER OF NOT LETTING THE HEART OF A MAN BE TAKEN AWAY FROM HIM IN THE UNDERWORLD

Says Osiris Ani, triumphant: "Turn thou back, O messenger of all the gods. Is it that thou art come to carry away my heart that lives? My heart that lives shall not be given unto thee. [As I] advance, the gods give ear unto my supplications, and they fall down upon their faces wheresoever they be."

Says Osiris Ani: "Hail, ye who carry away hearts, [hail] ye who steal hearts! ye have done. Homage to you, O ye lords of eternity, ye possessors of everlastingness, take ye not away this heart of Osiris Ani in your grasp, this heart of Osiris. And cause ye not evil words to spring up against it; because this heart of Osiris Ani is the heart of the one of many names, the mighty one whose words are his limbs, and who sends forth his heart to dwell in his body … heart of Osiris Ani is pleasant unto the gods; he is victorious, he has … power over it; he has not revealed what has been done unto it. He … got power over his own limbs. His heart obeys him, he is the lord thereof, it is in his body, and it shall never fall away therefrom. I, Osiris, the scribe Ani, victorious in peace, and triumphant in the beautiful Amenta and on the mountain of eternity, bid thee be obedient unto me in the underworld."

THE CHAPTER OF BREATHING THE AIR AND OF HAVING POWER OVER THE WATER IN THE UNDERWORLD

Says Osiris Ani: "Open to me! Who art thou then, and where goes thou? I am one of you. Who is it with thee? It is Merti. Separate thou from him, each from each, when thou enters the Mesqen. He lets me sail to the temple of the divine beings who have found their faces. The name of the boat is 'Assembler of Souls'; the name of the oars is 'Making the hair to stand on end'; the name of the hold is 'Good'; and the name of the rudder is 'Making straight for the middle' … Grant me vessels of milk together with cakes, loaves of bread, cups of drink and flesh in the temple of Anubis."

SCRIBE'S NOTE:

If this chapter be known [by Ani] he shall go in after having come forth from the underworld.

THE CHAPTER OF SNIFFING THE AIR AND OF GETTING POWER OVER THE WATERS IN THE UNDERWORLD

Says Osiris Ani: "Hail, sycamore tree of the goddess Nut! Grant thou to me of the water and the air that are in thee. I embrace thy throne that is in Unnu, and I watch and guard the Egg of the Great Cackler. It grows, I grow; it lives, I live; it sniffs the air, I sniff the air, I the Osiris Ani, in triumph."

THE CHAPTER OF NOT DYING A SECOND TIME IN THE UNDERWORLD

Says Osiris Ani: "My place of hiding is opened, my place of hiding is revealed! Light has shone in the darkness. The eye of Horus has ordered my coming into being, and the god Apuat has nursed me. I

The sun disk of the god Ra is raised into the sky by an ankh-sign (signifying life) and a djed-pillar (signifying stability and Osiris) while adored by Isis, Nephthys and baboons.

have hidden myself with you, O ye stars that never set. My brow is like unto that of Ra; my face is open; my heart is upon its throne; I utter words, and I know; in very truth, I am Ra himself. I am not treated with scorn, and violence is not done unto me. Thy father, the son of Nut, lives for thee. I am thy first-born, and I see thy mysteries. I am crowned like unto the king of the gods, and I shall not die a second time in the underworld."

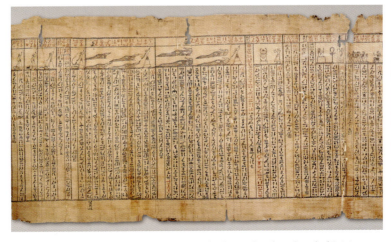

Spell 30 for stopping the heart betraying the deceased at the tribunal of Osiris, Iufankh's Book of the Dead.

THE CHAPTER OF NOT CORRUPTING IN THE UNDERWORLD

Says Osiris Ani: "O thou who art without motion like unto Osiris! O thou who art without motion like unto Osiris! O thou whose limbs are without motion like unto [those of] Osiris! Let not thy limbs be without motion, let them not corrupt, let

them not pass away, let them not decay; let it be done unto me even as if I were the god Osiris."

SCRIBE'S NOTE:

If this chapter be known by the Osiris Ani, he shall not corrupt in the underworld.

THE CHAPTER OF NOT PERISHING AND OF BECOMING ALIVE IN THE UNDERWORLD

Says Osiris Ani: "Hail, children of Shu! Hail, children of Shu, [children of] the place of the dawn, who as the children of light have gained possession of his crown. May I rise up and may I fare forth like Osiris."

THE CHAPTER OF NOT ENTERING THE BLOCK

Says Osiris Ani: "The four bones of my neck and of my back are joined together for me in heaven by Ra, the guardian of the earth. This was granted on the day when my rising up out of weakness upon my two feet was ordered, on the day when the hair was cut off. The bones of

Ouserhat drinking the water of paradise with his wife and mother in front of the goddess Nut (from a copy of a fresco from the Tomb of Ouserhat, Thebes, dating back to the reign of Seti I).

my neck and of my back have been joined together by Set and by the company of the gods, even as they were in the time that is past; may nothing happen to break them apart. Make ye [me] strong against my father's murderer. I have power over the two earths. Nut has joined together my bones, and [I] behold [them] as they were in the time that is past [and I] see [them] even in the same order as they were [when] the gods had not come into being in visible forms. I am Penti, I, Osiris the scribe Ani, triumphant, am the heir of the great gods."

THE CHAPTER OF NOT LETTING A MAN PASS OVER TO THE EAST IN THE UNDERWORLD

Says Osiris Ani: "Hail, manhood of Ra, which advances and beats down opposition; things that have been without movement for millions of years come into being through the god Baba. Hereby am I made stronger than the strong, and hereby have I more power than they who are mighty. And therefore neither shall I be borne away nor carried by force to the East, to take part in the festivals of the fiends; nor shall there [be given unto me] cruel gashes with knives, nor shall I be shut in on every side, nor gored by the horns [of the god Khepera]" ...

ANOTHER CHAPTER

[Says Osiris Ani]: "So then shall no evil things be done unto me by the fiends, neither shall I be gored by the horns [of Khepera]; and the manhood of Ra, which is the head of Osiris, shall not be swallowed up. Behold me, I enter into my homestead, and I reap the harvest. The gods speak with me. Gore thou not them, O Ra-khepera. In very truth sickness shall not arise in the eye of Tmu nor shall it be destroyed. Let me be brought to an end, may I not be carried into the East to take part in the festivals of the fiends who are my enemies; may no cruel gashes be made in me. I, Osiris, the scribe Ani, the teller of the divine offerings of all the gods, triumphant with happy victory, the lord to be revered, am not carried away into the East."

Nectanebo II offers incense (left) and a collar (right) to Osiris (360–343 BC).

THE CHAPTER OF NOT LETTING THE HEAD OF A MAN BE CUT OFF FROM HIM IN THE UNDERWORLD

Says Osiris Ani: "I am the great One, son of the great One; I am Fire, the son of Fire, to whom was given his head after it had been cut off. The head of Osiris was not carried away from him; let not the head of Osiris Ani be carried away from him. I have knit together my bones, I have made myself whole and sound; I have become young once more; I am Osiris, the Lord of eternity."

Tomb painting showing men carrying food as offerings to the gods (from the Tomb of Ti at Saqqara).

THE CHAPTER OF CAUSING THE SOUL TO BE UNITED TO ITS BODY IN THE UNDERWORLD

Says Osiris Ani: "Hail, thou god Annitu! Hail, O Runner, dwelling in thy hall! O thou great god, grant thou that my soul may come unto me from wheresoever it may be. If it would tarry, then bring thou unto me my soul from wheresoever it may be. [If] thou finds [me], O Eye of Horus, make me stand up like those beings who are like unto Osiris and who never lie down in death. Let not Osiris Ani, triumphant, triumphant, lie down in death in Annu, the land wherein souls are joined unto their bodies, even in thousands. My soul does bear away with it my victorious spirit wheresoever it goes … If it would tarry, grant thou that my soul may look upon my body. [If] thou finds [me], O Eye of Horus, make me stand up like unto those …

Hail, ye gods, who row in the boat of the lord of millions of years, who tow it above the underworld, who make it pass over the ways of Nu, who make souls enter into their glorified bodies, whose hands are filled with righteousness, and whose fingers grasp your sceptres, destroy ye the foe. The boat of the Sun rejoices, and the great god advances in peace. Behold [ye gods], grant that this soul of Osiris Ani may come forth triumphant before the gods, and triumphant before you, from the eastern horizon of heaven, to follow unto the place where it was yesterday, in peace, in peace, in Amenta. May he behold his body, may he rest in his glorified frame, may he never perish, and may his body never see corruption."

SCRIBE'S NOTE:

To be said over a golden [figure of a] soul inlaid with precious stones, which is to be placed on the neck of Osiris.

THE CHAPTER OF NOT LETTING THE SOUL OF A MAN BE CAPTIVE IN THE UNDERWORLD

Says Osiris Ani: "Hail thou who art exalted, thou who art adored, thou mighty one of souls, thou Ram (or Soul), possessor of terrible power,

Part of the Book of the Dead for Princess Nany. To the left appears the the lake of fire, which consumes the wicked.

who puts fear of thee into the hearts of the gods, thou who art crowned upon thy mighty throne! It is he who makes the path for the khu and for the soul of Osiris Ani. I am furnished [with that which I need], I am a khu furnished [with that which I need], I have made my way unto the place wherein are Ra and Hathor."

Coffin of Denytenamun, Priest of Amun. The coffin depicts the sun-god Ra as a solar disk on a boat. Osiris appears below in his distinctive crown.

SCRIBE'S NOTE:

If this chapter be known, Ani shall become like a shining being, fully equipped in the underworld. He shall not be stopped at any door in the underworld from going in and coming out millions of times.

THE CHAPTER OF OPENING THE TOMB TO THE SOUL OF THE SHADOW, OF COMING FORTH BY DAY AND OF GETTING POWER OVER THE LEGS

Says Osiris, the scribe Ani, triumphant: "The place of bondage is opened, that which was shut is opened, and the place of bondage is opened unto my soul [according to the bidding of] the eye of Horus. I have bound and established glories upon the brow of Ra. [My] steps are made long, [my] thighs are lifted up; I have passed along the great path, and my limbs are strong. I am Horus, the avenger of his father, and I bring the urerit crown to rest upon its place. The path of souls is opened [to my soul]."

"My soul sees the great god within the boat of Ra on the day of souls. My soul is in the front among those who tell the years. Come, the eye of Horus, which establishes glories upon the brow of Ra and rays of light upon the faces of those who are with the limbs of Osiris, has delivered my soul. O shut ye not in my soul, fetter ye not my shade, may it behold the great god within the shrine on the day of the judgement of souls, may it repeat the words of Osiris. May those beings whose dwelling places are hidden, who fetter the limbs of Osiris, who fetter the souls of the khu, who shut in the shade[s] of the dead and can do evil unto me – may they do no evil unto me, may they turn away their path from me. Thy heart is with thee; may my soul and my khu be prepared against their attack. May I sit down among the great rulers who dwell in their abodes; may my soul not be set in bondage by those who fetter the limbs of Osiris, and who fetter souls, and who shut in the shade[s] of the dead. The place that thou possesses, is it not heaven?"

A harp player worships the solar god Horus, son of Osiris and Isis.

SCRIBE'S NOTE:

If this chapter be known, he shall come forth by day and his soul shall not be shut in.

THE CHAPTER OF WALKING WITH TWO LEGS AND OF COMING FORTH UPON EARTH

Says Osiris Ani: "Thou has done all thy work, O Seker, thou has done all thy work, O Seker, in thy dwelling place within my legs in the underworld. I shine above the Leg of the Sky, I come forth from heaven; I recline with the glorified spirits. Alas! I am weak and feeble; alas! I am weak and feeble. I walk. I am weak and feeble in the presence of those who gnash with teeth in the underworld, I Osiris, the scribe Ani, triumphant in peace."

THE CHAPTER OF PASSING THROUGH AMENTA AND OF COMING FORTH BY DAY

Says Osiris Ani: "The hour opens; the head of Thoth is sealed up;

perfect is the eye of Horus. I have delivered the eye of Horus that shines with splendours on the forehead of Ra, the father of the gods. I am the same Osiris, dwelling in Amenta. Osiris knows his day and that he shall not live therein; nor shall I live therein. I am the Moon among the gods; I shall not come to an end. Stand up, therefore, O Horus; Osiris has counted thee among the gods."

A carved and painted relief of priests in procession carrying a model of a sacred barque (boat). The deck structure would hide a statue of the god Amun.

THE CHAPTER OF COMING FORTH BY DAY AND OF LIVING AFTER DEATH

Says Osiris Ani: "Hail, Only One, shining from the Moon! Hail, Only One, shining from the Moon!

Grant that this Osiris Ani may come forth among the multitudes that are round about thee; let him be established as a dweller among the shining ones; and let the underworld be opened unto him. And behold Osiris, Osiris Ani shall come forth by day to do his will upon earth among the living."

THE CHAPTER OF COMING FORTH BY DAY, HAVING PASSED THROUGH THE TOMB

Says Osiris Ani: "Hail Soul, thou mighty one of strength! Verily I am here, I have come, I behold thee. I have passed through the underworld, I have seen [my] father Osiris, I have scattered the gloom of night. I am his beloved one. I have come; behold my father Osiris. I

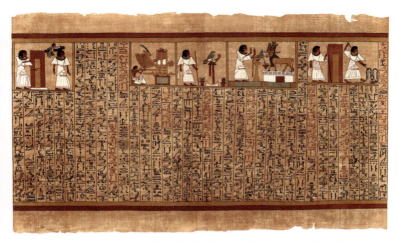

Ani progressing through the Other World. At the top left, Ani passes through a gate and two parts of his spirit or 'soul' – the ka and the ba-bird emerge the other side (from the Papyrus of Ani, 1250 BC).

have stabbed Set to the heart. I have done the things [needed] by my father Osiris. I have opened every way in heaven and upon earth. I am the son beloved of his father Osiris. I have become a ruler, I have become glorious, I am furnished [with what I need]. Hail, all ye gods, and all ye shining ones, make ye a way for me, the Osiris, the scribe Ani, triumphant."

Relief of a solar boat carrying Ra (as Nefer-Tum the setting sun). Mortuary Temple of Ramesses III, Medinat Habu, ca. 12th century BC.

THE CHAPTER OF MAKING A MAN RETURN TO SEE AGAIN HIS HOME UPON EARTH

Says Osiris Ani: "I am the Lion-god coming forth with strides. I have shot forth arrows, I have wounded [the prey], I have wounded the prey. I am the Eye of Horus; I have opened the eye of Horus in his hour. I am come unto the furrows. Let Osiris Ani come in peace."

ANOTHER CHAPTER OF ONE WHO COMES FORTH BY DAY AGAINST HIS FOES IN THE UNDERWORLD

Says Osiris Ani: "I have divided the heavens, I have passed through the horizon, I have traversed the earth, [following] upon his footsteps. I am borne away by the mighty and shining ones because, behold, I am furnished with millions of years that have magic virtues. I eat with my mouth, I chew with my jaws; and, behold, I am the god who is the lord of the underworld: May there be given unto me, Osiris Ani, that which abides for ever without corruption."

A HYMN OF PRAISE TO RA WHEN HE RISES UPON THE HORIZON AND WHEN HE SETS IN THE [LAND OF] LIFE

Says Osiris, the scribe Ani: "Homage to thee, O Ra, when thou rises [as] Tmu-Heru-khuti (Harmachis), thou art adored [by me] when thy beauties are before mine eyes, and when thy shining rays [fall] upon my body. Thou goes forth in peace in the sektet boat with [fair] winds, and thy heart is glad; [thou goes forth] in the atet boat, and its heart is glad. Thou strides over the heavens in peace, and thy foes are cast down; the never-resting stars sing hymns of praise unto thee, and the stars that never set glorify thee as thou sinks in the horizon of Manu, O thou who art beautiful in the two parts of heaven, thou lord who lives and art established, O my lord! Homage to thee, O thou who art Ra when thou rises, and Tmu when thou sets in beauty. Thou rises and shines upon the back of thy mother [the sky], O thou who art crowned king of the gods. Nut does homage unto thee, and everlasting and never-changing order embraces thee at morn and at eve. Thou strides over the heaven, being glad of heart, and the Lake Testes is at peace. The Fiend has fallen to the ground; his arms and his hands have been hewn off, and the knife has severed the joints of his body. Ra has a fair wind; the sektet boat goes forth and sailing along it comes into port. The gods of the south and of the north, of the west and of the east praise thee, from whom all forms of life came into being. Thou sends forth the word, and the earth is flooded with silence, O thou only One, who lives in heaven before ever the earth and the mountains were made. O Runner, Lord, only One, thou maker of things that are, thou has moulded the tongue of the company of the gods, thou has drawn forth whatsoever comes from the waters, and thou springs up from them over the flooded land of the Lake of Horus. Make me sniff the air that comes forth from thy nostrils, and the north wind that comes forth from thy mother [the sky]. Make thou glorious my shining form, O Osiris, make thou strong my soul. Thou art worshipped in peace, O lord of the gods, thou art exalted by reason of thy wondrous works. Shine with thy rays of light upon my body day by day, upon me, Osiris, the scribe, the teller of the divine offerings of all the gods, the overseer of the granary of the lords of Abydos, the royal scribe in truth, who loves him (Ra); Ani, triumphant in peace."

THE SOLAR LITANY

A HYMN OF PRAISE

O Osiris, lord of eternity, Un-nefer, Horus of the two horizons, whose forms are manifold, whose creations are without number, Ptah-Seker-Tem in Annu, the lord of the tomb, and the creator of Memphis and of the gods, the guide of the underworld, whom [the gods] glorify when thou sets in Nut. Isis embraces thee in peace, and she drives away the fiends from the mouth of thy paths. Thou turns thy face upon Amenta, thou makes the world shine as with smu metal. The dead rise up to behold thee, they breathe the air and they look upon thy face when the disc shines on its horizon; their hearts are at peace for that they behold thee, O thou who art eternity and everlastingness."

Ani and his wife, Tutu, making offerings to Osiris, from the Papyrus of Ani (sheet 36).

"Homage to thee, [O lord of] starry deities in An, and of heavenly beings in Kheraba; thou god Unti, who art more glorious than the gods who are hidden in Annu.

"Homage to thee, O An in Antes, Horus, thou dweller in both horizons, with long strides thou strides over heaven, O thou who dwells in both horizons.

"Homage to thee, O soul of everlastingness, thou Soul who dwells in Tattu, Un-nefer, son of Nut; thou art lord of Akert.

"Homage to thee in thy dominion over Tattu; the urerit crown is established upon thy head; thou art the One whose strength is in himself, and thou dwells in peace in Tattu.

Ancient Egyptian bas relief sculpture showing the Pharaoh Seti I with an offering for the gods (Temple of Osiris, Abydos).

"Homage to thee, O lord of the acacia tree, the sektet boat is set upon its sledge; thou turns back the Fiend, the worker of evil, and thou causes the utchat to rest upon its seat.

"Homage to thee, O thou who art mighty in thine hour, thou great and mighty god, dweller in Anrutf, lord of eternity and creator of everlastingness; thou art the lord of Suten-henen.

"Homage to thee, O thou who rests upon Right and Truth, thou art the lord of Abtu, and thy limbs are joined unto Ta-sert; thou art he to whom fraud and guile are hateful.Homage to thee, O thou who art within thy boat, thou brings Hapi (the Nile) forth from his source; the light shines upon thy body, and thou art the dweller in Nekhen.

"Homage to thee, O creator of the gods, thou King of the North and of the South;

O Osiris, victorious, ruler of the world in thy gracious seasons; thou art the lord of the world.

"O grant thou unto me a path whereon I may pass in peace, for I am just and true; I have not spoken lies wittingly, nor have I done anything whatsoever with deceit."

A HYMN OF PRAISE TO RA WHEN HE RISES IN THE EASTERN PART OF THE HEAVEN

They who are in his train rejoice, and lo! Osiris Ani in triumph says "Hail, thou disc, thou lord of rays, who rises in the horizon day by day. Shine thou with thy beams of light upon the face of Osiris Ani, who is victorious: for he sings hymns of praise unto thee at dawn, and he makes thee set at eventide with words of adoration. May the soul of Osiris Ani, the triumphant one, come forth with thee from heaven, may he go forth in the matet boat, may he come into port in the sektet boat, may he cleave his path among the never-resting stars in the heavens."

Osiris Ani, being at peace and in triumph, adores his lord, the lord of eternity, saying: "Homage to thee, O Horus of the two horizons, who art Khepera the self-created; when thou rises on the horizon and sheds thy beams of light upon the lands of the North and the South thou art beautiful, ye beautiful, and all the gods rejoice when they behold thee, the King of heaven. The goddess Nebt-Unnet is established upon thy head; her portions of the south and of the north are upon thy brow; she takes her place before thee. The god Thoth is established in the bows of thy boat to destroy utterly all thy foes. (Those who dwell in the underworld come forth to meet thee, bowing in homage as they come towards thee, and to behold [thy] beautiful image. And I have come before thee that I may be with thee to behold thy disc every day. May I not be shut in the tomb, may I not be turned back, may the limbs of my body be made new again when I view thy beauties, even as do all thy favoured ones, because I am one of those who worshipped thee while they lived upon earth. May I come into the land of eternity, may I come even into the everlasting land, for behold, O my lord, this has thou ordained for me."

And lo, Osiris Ani, triumphant in peace, the triumphant one, says: "Homage to thee, O thou who rises in thy horizon as Ra, thou art established by a law that changes not nor can it be altered. Thou passes over the sky, and every face watches thee and thy course, for thou has been hidden from their gaze. Thou shows thyself at dawn and at eventide day by day. The sektet boat, wherein is thy majesty, goes forth with might; thy beams shine upon [all] faces; [the number] of thy yellow rays cannot be known, nor can thy bright beams be told. The lands of the gods, and the colours of the eastern lands of Punt, must be seen, ere that which is hidden [in thee] may be measured [by man]. Alone and by thyself thou manifests thyself [when] thou comes into being above Nu. May Ani advance, even as thou advances; may he never cease [to go forward], even as thy majesty ceases not [to go forward], even though it be for a moment; for with strides does thou in one little moment pass over the spaces that would need hundreds of thousands and millions of years [for man to pass over; this] thou does, and then does thou sink down. Thou puts an end to the hours of the night,

The sun passes through the sky goddess Nut (from the lid of the sarcophagus coffin of Djedhor, 4th century BC).

Nut, goddess of the sky

and thou does number them, even thou; thou ends them in thine own appointed season, and the earth becomes light. Thou sets thyself before thy handiwork in the likeness of Ra; thou rises in the horizon."

Osiris, the scribe Ani, triumphant, declares his praise of thee when thou shines, and when thou rises at dawn he cries in his joy at thy birth: "Thou art crowned with the majesty of thy beauties; thou moulds thy limbs as thou advances, and thou brings them forth without birth-pangs in the form of Ra, as thou climbs up into the upper air. Grant thou that I may come unto the heaven that is everlasting, and unto the mountain [where dwell] thy favoured ones. May I be joined unto those shining beings, holy and perfect, who are in the underworld; and may I come forth with them to behold thy beauties when thou shines at eventide and goes to thy mother Nut."

"Thou places thy disc in the west, and my two hands are [raised] in adoration [of thee] when thou sets as a living being. Behold, thou art the maker of eternity, and thou art adored [when] thou sets in the heavens. I have given my heart unto thee without wavering, O thou who art mightier than the gods."

Osiris Ani, triumphant, says:
"A hymn of praise to thee, O thou who rises like unto gold, and who floods the world with light on the day of thy birth. Thy mother gives thee birth upon [her] hand, and thou gives light unto the course of the disc. O thou mighty Light, who shines in the heavens, thou strengthens the generations of men with the Nile flood, and causes gladness in all lands, and in all cities, and in all the temples. Thou art glorious by reason of thy splendours, and thou makes strong thy ka with hu and tchefa foods. O thou who art the mighty one of victories, thou who art the Power of [all] Powers, who makes strong thy throne against the powers of wickedness, who art glorious in majesty in the sektet boat, and who art exceedingly mighty in the atet boat, make thou glorious Osiris Ani with victory in the underworld; grant thou that in the underworld he may be void of sin. I pray thee to put away [his] faults

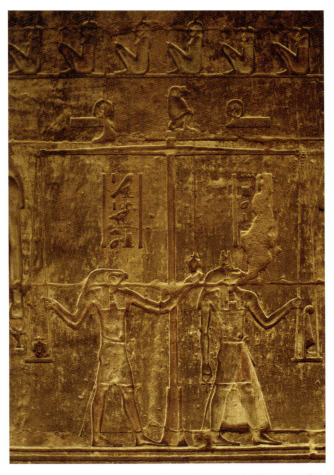

The gods Horus and Anubis (interior of the Ptolemaic temple of Hathor and Maat, Deir el-Medina).

behind thee; grant that he may be one of thy venerable servants who are with the shining ones; may he be joined unto the souls that are in Ta-sert; and may he journey into the Sekhet-Aru by a prosperous and happy path, he the Osiris, the scribe Ani, triumphant.

Thou shall come forth into heaven, thou shall pass over the sky, thou shall be joined unto the starry deities. Praises shall be offered unto thee in thy boat, thou shall be hymned in the diet boat, thou shall behold Ra within his shrine, thou shall set together with his disc day by day, thou shall see the ant fish when it springs into being in the waters of turquoise, and thou shall see the abtu fish in his hour. May it come to pass that the Evil One shall fall when he lays a snare to destroy me, and may the joints of his neck and of his back be cut in sunder."

"Ra [sails] with a fair wind, and the sektet boat draws on and comes into port. The mariners of Ra rejoice, and the heart of Nebt-ankh is glad, for the enemy of her lord has fallen to the ground. Thou shall behold Horus on the watch [in the boat], and Thoth and Maat upon either side of him. All the gods rejoice when they behold Ra coming in peace to make the hearts of the shining ones live. May Osiris Ani, triumphant, the scribe of the divine offerings of the lords of Thebes, be with them."

THE CHAPTER OF THE NEW MOON

TO BE SAID ON THE DAY OF THE MONTH

Osiris Ani, the scribe, triumphant in peace, triumphant, says:

"Ra rises in his horizon, and the company of his gods follow after the god when he appears from his secret place, when he shows strength and brings himself forth from the eastern horizon of heaven at the word of the goddess Nut. They rejoice at the journeys of Ra, the Ancient One; the Great One rolls along in his course. Thy joints are knitted together, O Ra, within thy shrine. Thou breathes the winds, thou draws in the breezes, thou makes thy jaw bones to eat in thy dwelling on the day when thou scents right and truth. Thou turns aside the godlike followers [who] sail after the sacred boat, in order that they may return again unto the mighty ones according to thy word. Thou numbers thy bones, thou gathers together thy members; thou turns thy face towards the beautiful Amenta; thou comes thither renewed day by day. Behold, thou image of gold, who possesses the splendours of the disc of heaven, thou lord of terror; thou rolls along and art renewed day by day. Hail, there is rejoicing in the heavenly horizon. May the gods who dwell in heaven ascribe praises unto Osiris Ani, when they behold him in triumph, as unto Ra. May Osiris, the scribe Ani, be a

The god Ra-Harakhti (centre), from a papyrus of the Book of the Dead (c. 1000 BC).

prince who is known by the urerit crown; and may the meat offerings and the drink offerings of Osiris Ani, triumphant, be apportioned unto him; may he wax exceedingly strong in his body; and may he be the chief of those who are in the presence of Ra. May Osiris, the scribe Ani, triumphant, be strong upon earth and in the world under the earth; and O Osiris, scribe Ani, triumphant, may thou rise up strengthened like unto Ra day by day. Osiris Ani, triumphant, shall not tarry, nor shall he rest without motion in the earth for ever. Clearly, clearly shall he see with his two eyes, and with his two ears shall be hear what is right and true. Osiris, the scribe Ani, triumphant, comes back, comes back from Annu; Osiris Ani, triumphant, is as Ra when he ranges the oars among the followers of Nu.

"Osiris Ani, triumphant, has not revealed what he has seen, he has not, he has not told again what he has heard in the house that is hidden. Hail, there are shouts of joy to Osiris Ani, triumphant, for he is a god and the flesh of Ra, he is in the boat of Nu, and his ka is well pleased according to the will of the god. Osiris Ani, triumphant, is in peace, he is triumphant like unto Horus, and he is mighty because he has diverse forms."

SCRIBE'S NOTES:

These words shall be recited over a boat seven cubits in length, and painted green for the godlike rulers. Then shall thou make a heaven of stars washed and purified with natron and incense. Behold, thou shall make an image of Ra upon a table of stone painted yellow, and it shall be placed in the front of the boat. Behold, thou shall make an image of the dead man whom thou will make perfect in strength in the boat; and thou shall make it travel in the divine boat of Ra, and Ra himself will look upon it therein. Thou shall show it to no man but thyself, or to thy father or to thy son; let them watch with their faces, and he shall be seen in the underworld as a messenger of Ra.

A HYMN OF PRAISE TO RA ON THE DAY OF THE MONTH WHEREON HE SAILS IN THE BOAT

[Osiris, the scribe Ani, says]: "Homage to thee, O thou who art in thy boat! Thou rises, thou rises, thou shines with thy rays, and thou has made humankind rejoice for millions of years according to thy will. Thou shows thy face unto the beings whom thou has created, O Khepera, in thy boat. Thou has overthrown Apep. O ye children of Seb, overthrow ye the foes of Osiris Ani, triumphant, destroy ye the adversaries of righteousness from the boat of Ra. Horus shall cut off your heads in heaven in the likeness of ducks; ye shall fall down upon the earth and become beasts, and into the water in the likeness of fishes.

"[Osiris, the scribe Ani] destroys every hostile fiend, male and female, whether he passes through heaven, [or] appears upon earth, or comes forth upon the water, or passes along before the starry deities;

Stela showing the solar boat carrying the Sun Disk with Ra holding an ankh. Before the deceased stands Isis-Hathor, with a solar disk between cow's horns.

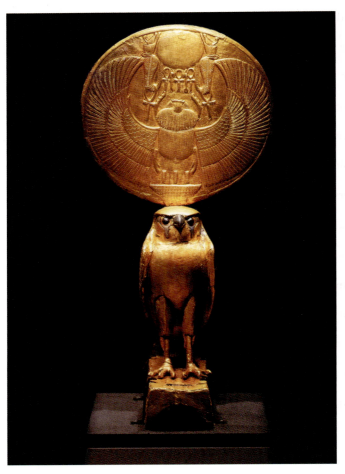

The Solar Hawk: a gilded wooden statue of the god Horus with the sun on its head, from Tutankhamun's tomb treasures.

and Thoth strengthens them … coming forth from Anreti. Osiris, the scribe Ani, is silent, and becomes the second of Ra. Behold thou the god, the great slaughterer, greatly to be feared, he washes in your blood, he bathes in your gore; Osiris, the scribe Ani, destroys them from the boat of his father Ra-Horus. The mother Isis gives birth unto Osiris, the scribe Ani, triumphant, whose heart lives, and Nephthys nurses him; even as they did for Horus, who drove back the fiends of Sut. They saw the urerit crown established upon his head, and they fell down upon their faces. Behold, O ye shining ones, ye men and gods, ye damned ones, when ye behold Osiris Ani, triumphant like unto Horus and adored by reason of the urerit crown, fall ye down upon your faces; for Osiris Ani is victorious over his foes in the heavens above and [on the earth] beneath, in the presence of the godlike rulers, of all the gods and goddesses."

SCRIBE'S NOTES:

These words shall be recited over a great hawk that has the white crown set upon his head. Then shall the names of Tmu, Shu, Tefnut, Seb, Nut, Osiris, Isis, Nephthys be written with green colour upon a new table, anointed with unguents and placed in a boat together with a figure of the dead man. Then shall they put incense upon the fire, and set ducks to be roasted. This is a rite of Ra when his boat comes; and it shall cause the dead man to go with Ra into every place wheresoever he sails, and the foes of Ra shall be slaughtered in very truth. The Chapter of the sektet boat shall be recited on the sixth day of the festival.

THE CHAPTER OF GOING UNTO THE GODLIKE RULERS OF OSIRIS

Osiris, the scribe Ani, triumphant, says:

"My soul has built for me a dwelling place in Tattu. I have waxed strong in the town Pe. I have ploughed [my] fields in all my forms, and my palm tree stands therein like unto the god Amsu. I eat not that which I abominate, I eat not that which I loathe; that which I abominate

I abominate, and I feed not upon filth. There are food offerings and meat for those who shall not be destroyed thereby. I raise not up myself on my two arms unto any abomination, I walk not thereupon with my shoes, because my bread is [made] from white grain, and my ale from the red barley of the Nile. The sektet boat and the atet boat bring them unto me, and I feed upon them under the trees, whose beautiful branches I myself know. How glorious do I make the white crown

Relief depicting an offerer with food (New Kingdom period, Karnak temple complex).

[when] I lift up the uraei! Hail, guardian of the door, who gives peace unto the two lands, bring thou unto me those who make offerings! Grant that I may lift up the earth; that the shining ones may open their arms unto me; that the company of the gods may speak with the words of the shining ones unto Osiris Ani; that the hearts of the gods may direct [him]; and that they may make him powerful in heaven among the gods who have taken unto themselves visible forms. Yea, let every god and every goddess whom he passes make Osiris, the scribe Ani, triumphant at the new year. He feeds upon hearts and consumes them when he comes forth from the east. He has been judged by the forefather of Light. He is a shining one arrayed in heaven among the mighty ones. The food of Osiris, the scribe Ani, triumphant, is even the cakes and ale that are made for their mouths. I go in through the disc, I come out through the god Ahui. I speak with the followers of the gods, I speak with the disc, I speak with the shining ones, and the disc grants me victory in the blackness of night within Mehurt near unto his forehead. Behold, I am with Osiris, and I proclaim that which

he tells forth among the mighty ones. He speaks unto me the words of men, and I listen and I tell again unto him the words of the gods. I, Osiris Ani, triumphant, come even as one who is equipped for the journey. Thou raises up [right and truth] for those who love them. I am a shining one clothed in power, mightier than any other shining one."

HERE BEGIN THE CHAPTERS OF MAKING TRANSFORMATIONS: THE CHANGING INTO A SWALLOW

Says Osiris Ani, triumphant: "I am the swallow, [I am] the swallow, [I am] the scorpion, the daughter of Ra. Hail, ye gods, whose scent is sweet; hail, ye gods, whose scent is sweet! Hail, thou Flame, which comes forth from the horizon! Hail, thou who art in the city. May the Guardian of the Bight lead me on. O stretch out up unto me thine bands that I may be able to pass my days in the Island of Flame. I have fared forth with my warrant. I have come with the power thereof. Let the doors be opened unto me. How shall I tell what I have seen therein? Horus was like unto the prince of the sacred bark, and the throne of his father was given unto him. Sut, the son of Nut, also got the fall that he wrought for Horus. He who is in Sekhem passed judgement upon me. I stretched out my hands and my arms unto Osiris. I have passed on to judgement, and I have come that I may speak; grant that I may pass on and deliver my message. I enter in, having been judged; I come out at the door of Neb-er-tcher magnified and glorified. I am found pure at the great place of passage [of souls]. I have put away my faults. I have done away my offences. I have cast out the sins that were a part of me. I, even I, am pure, I, even I, am mighty. O ye doorkeepers, I have made my way [unto you]. I am like unto you. I have come forth by day. I have walked with my legs, and I have got the power of the footstep wherewith do walk the shining ones of light. I, even I, know the hidden ways to the doors of the Field of Aru; and, though my body be buried, yet let me rise up; and may I come forth and overthrow all my foes upon earth."

CHAPTER OF CHANGING INTO A GOLDEN HAWK

Says Osiris Ani: "May I, even I, arise in the seshet chamber, like unto

A limestone relief plaque showing two swallows (400–30 BC).

Relief plaque depicting the god Horus as a falcon (Ptolemaic Period, 664–30 BC).

a hawk of gold coming forth from his egg. May I fly and may I hover as a hawk, with a back seven cubits wide, and with wings made of emeralds of the south. May I come forth from the sektet boat, and may my heart be brought unto me from the mountain of the east. May I alight on the atet boat, and may those who are in their companies be brought unto me, bowing down as they come. May I rise, may I gather myself together as the beautiful golden hawk [that has] the head of a bennu bird. May I enter into the presence of Ra daily to hear his words, and may I sit down among the mighty gods of Nut. May a homestead be made ready for me, and may offerings of food and drink be put before me therein. May I eat therein; may I become a shining one therein; may I be filled therein to, my heart's fullest desire; may sacred wheat be given unto me to eat. May I, by myself, get power over the guardian of my head."

THE CHAPTER OF CHANGING INTO A SACRED HAWK

Says Osiris Ani: "Hail, thou mighty one, come unto Tattu. Make thou my paths, and let me pass round [to visit] my thrones. Make me renew myself and make me wax strong. Grant that I may be feared, and make me a terror. May the gods of the underworld fear me, and may they fight for me in their habitations. Let not him that would do harm unto me draw nigh unto me. Let me walk through the house of darkness. May I, the feeble, clothe and cover myself; and may they (the gods) not do the like unto me. Hail, ye gods who hear my speech! Hail, ye rulers who are among the followers of Osiris. Be ye therefore silent, O ye gods, [when] the god speaks with me; he hears what is right and true. What I speak unto him, do thou also speak, O Osiris. Grant thou that I may go round my course according to the order that comes forth from thy mouth concerning me. May I see thy forms; may I be able to understand thy will. Grant that I may come forth, that I may get power over my legs, and that I may be like unto Neb-er-tcher upon his throne. May the gods of the underworld fear me, and may they fight for me in their habitations. Grant thou that I may pass on my way with the godlike ones who rise up. May I be set up upon my resting place like unto the Lord of Life; may I be joined unto Isis, the divine Lady. May the gods make me strong against him that would do harm unto me, and may no one come to see me fall helpless. May I pass over the paths, may I come into the furthermost parts of heaven. I entreat for speech with Seb, I make supplication unto Hu and unto Neb-er-tcher that the gods of the underworld may fear me, and that they may fight for me in their habitations, when they see that thou has provided me with the fowl of the air and the fish of the sea."

"I am one of those shining ones who live in rays of light. I have made my form like unto the form [of the god] who comes out and manifests himself in Tattu; for I have become worthy of honour by reason of his honour, and he has spoken unto thee of the things that concern me. Surely, he has made the fear of me [go forth], and has created terror of me! The gods of the underworld fear me, and they fight for me [in their habitations]. I, in very truth I am a shining one and a dweller in light, who has been created and who has come into being from the body of the god. I am one of the shining ones who dwell in light,

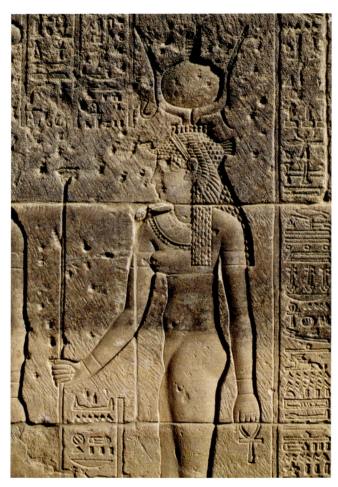

Relief of Isis, from the Temple of Arensnuphis, Philae, Agilkia Island, Aswan.

whom Tmu himself has created, and who have come into being from the eyelashes of his eye. He creates and glorifies and makes noble the faces of those who live with him. Behold, the only One in Nu! They do homage unto him as he comes forth from the horizon, and they strike fear of him into the gods and into the shining ones who have come into being with him."

"I am the One among the worms that the eye of the Lord, the only One, has created. And lo! before Isis was, and when Horus was not yet, I had waxed strong, and flourished. I had grown old, and I had become greater than they who were among the shining ones who had come into being with him, and I, even I, arose in the form of a sacred hawk, and Horus made me worthy in the form of his own soul, to take possession of all that belongs unto Osiris in the underworld. The double Lion-god, the warder of the things that belong to the house of the nemmes crown that is in his hiding place, says unto me: 'Get thee back to the heights of heaven, seeing that through Horus thou has become glorified in thy form; the nemmes crown is not for thee; thou has speech even unto the ends of heaven.' I, the guardian, take possession of the things that belong to Horus and Osiris in the underworld. Horus tells aloud unto me that which his father had said concerning me in years [gone by], on the day of the burial [of Osiris]. I have given unto thee the nemmes of the double Lion-god that I possess, that thou may pass onwards and may travel over the path of heaven, and that they who dwell on the confines of the horizon may see thee, and that the gods of the underworld may fear thee and may fight for thee in their habitations. The god Auhet is of them. The gods, the lords of the boundaries of heaven, they who are the warders of the shrine of the lord, the only One, have fallen before my words, have fallen down before [my] words."

"Hail! He that is exalted upon his tomb is on my side, and he has bound upon my head the nemmes crown. The double Lion-god has decreed it, the god Auhet has made a way for me. I, even I, am exalted, and the double Lion-god has bound the nemmes crown on me, and my head covering has been given unto me. He has established my heart through his strength and through his great might, and I shall not fall through Shu. I am Hetep, the lord of the two uraei, the being who is adored. I know the shining god, and his breath is in my body. I shall not be driven

Sandstone architrave showing two lion gods and the god Amon as a Ram (ca. 200 BC, Musawarat es Sufra, Sudan).

A relief showing the goddess Mut (left) and god Horus (right), each side of Seti I at the Mortuary Temple of Seti I, Abydos.

back by the Bull that causes men to tremble, but I shall come daily into the house of the double Lion-god, and I shall come forth therefrom into the house of Isis. I shall behold sacred things that are hidden, there shall be done unto me holy hidden rites, I shall see what is there; my words shall make full the majesty of Shu, and they shall drive away evil hap (fortune). I, even I, am Horus who dwells in splendours. I have gained power over his crown, I have gained power over his radiance, and I have travelled over the remotest parts of heaven. Horus is upon his throne, Horus is upon his seat. My face is like that of a divine hawk. I am one who has been armed by his lord. I have come forth from Tattu. I have seen Osiris, I have risen up on either side of him. Nut [has shrouded me]. The gods behold me, and I have beheld the gods. The eye of Horus has consumed me, who dwell in darkness. The gods stretch forth their arms unto me. I rise up, I have mastery, and I drive back evil that opposes me. The gods open unto me the holy way, they see my form, and they hear my words that I utter in their presence."

"O ye gods of the underworld, who set yourselves up against me, and who resist the mighty ones, the stars that never set have led me on my way. I have passed along the holy paths of the hemtet chamber unto your lord, the exceedingly mighty and terrible Soul. Horus has commanded that ye lift up your faces to look upon me. I have risen up in the likeness of a divine hawk, and Horus has set me apart in the likeness of his own soul, to take possession of that which belongs unto Osiris in the underworld. I have passed along the way, I have travelled on and I have come even among those who live in their hiding places and who guard the house of Osiris. I speak unto them of his power and I make them know the terrible power of him that is provided with two horns [to fight] against Sut; and they know who has carried off the sacred food that the power of Tmu had brought for him."

"The gods of the underworld have proclaimed a happy coming for me. O Ye who live in your hiding places and who guard the house of Osiris, and who have magnified your names, grant ye that I may come unto you. I bind together and I gather up your powers, and I order the strength of the paths of those who guard the horizon of the hemtet of heaven. I have established their habitations for Osiris, I have ordered his ways, I have done what has been bidden. I have come forth from Tattu, I have beheld Osiris, I have spoken unto him concerning the things of his son, the divine Prince whom he loves. There is a wound in the heart of Set, and I have seen him who is without life. O, I have made them know the plans of the gods that Horus has devised at the bidding of his father Osiris."

"Hail, lord, thou most terrible and mighty soul! Let me come, even me, let me lift myself up! I have opened and passed through the underworld. I have opened the paths of the warders of heaven and of the warders of the earth. I have not been driven back by them; and I have lifted up thy face, O lord of eternity."

THE CHAPTER OF BEING AMONG THE COMPANY OF THE GODS AND OF BEING CHANGED INTO THE PRINCE OF THE GODLIKE RULERS

[The deceased] say: "Homage to thee, O Tmu, lord of heaven, thou creator of things that are and that come forth from the earth; who makes that which is sown come into being, the lord of things that shall be, the begetter of the gods, the great god who made himself, the lord of life who makes humankind flourish. Homage to you, O ye lords of creation, ye pure being whose abodes are hidden. Homage to you, O ye lords of eternity, whose forms are hidden, and whose dwelling places are unknown. Homage to you, O ye gods who dwell in the abode of the flooded lands. Homage to you, O ye gods who live in the underworld. Homage to you, O ye gods who dwell in heaven. Grant ye that I may come [unto you], for I know you. I am pure, I am holy, I am mighty, I have a soul, I have become powerful, I am glorious; I have brought unto you perfume and incense, and natron. Blot out from your hearts whatsoever ye have in them against me. I have come, having done away

Here the temple-servant of Amun, Irtihareru, son of the temple-servant of Amun Ankhnidi and the lady of the house Tatjenfi, adores Osiris on the right side and Atum on the left side (ca. 750–525 BC).

The god Sobek in his Nile crocodile form as seen on the wall of the Temple of Kom Ombo.

all the evil that dwells in your hearts against me, I have made an end of all the sin that I committed against you; I have brought unto you that which is good, I have made that which is right and true come unto you. I, even I, know you, I know your names, I know your forms that are not known, that come into being with you. I have come unto you.

"I have risen among men like unto the god, living among the gods. I am strong before you like unto the god who is exalted upon his resting place; when he comes, the gods rejoice, and goddesses and mortal women are glad when they behold him. I have come unto you. I have risen upon the throne of Ra, I sit upon my seat in the horizon. I receive offerings upon my altar, I drink offerings at eventide as one made noble by the lord of mortals. I am exalted even as the holy god, the lord of the great House. The gods rejoice when they see him in his beautiful manifestation on the body of Nut, who gives birth unto him daily."

THE CHAPTER OF CHANGING INTO SETA

Osiris Ani, triumphant, says: "I am the serpent Seta, whose years are many. I lie down and I am born day by day. I am the serpent Seta that dwells in the limits of the earth. I lie down, I am born, I renew myself, I grow young day by day."

THE CHAPTER OF CHANGING INTO A CROCODILE

Says Osiris Ani, triumphant:

"I am the crocodile that dwells in terror, I am the sacred crocodile and I cause destruction. I am the great fish in Kamui. I am the lord to whom homage is paid in Sekhem; and Osiris Ani is the lord to whom homage is paid in Sekhem."

THE CHAPTER OF CHANGING INTO PTAH

Says Osiris Ani, triumphant: "I eat bread, I drink ale, I put on apparel, I fly like a hawk, I cackle like a goose, and I alight upon the path hard by the hill of the dead on the festival of the great Being. That which is abominable, that which is abominable, I have not eaten; and that which is foul I have not swallowed. That which my ka abominates has not entered into my body. I have lived according to the knowledge of the glorious gods. I live and I get strength from their bread, I get strength when I eat it beneath the shade of the tree of Hathor, my lady. I make an offering, and I make bread in Tattu, and oblations

The deceased worships the sacred image of a Bennu bird (from the tomb of Inherkhau, in the Asasif necropolis, Luxor).

in Annu. I array myself in the robe of the goddess Matait, and I rise up and I sit down wheresoever my heart desires. My head is like unto the head of Ra; when my limbs are gathered together, I am like unto

Mesu smelling a lotus (ca. 1525–1504 BC)

Tmu. The four regions of Ra are the limits of the earth. I come forth; my tongue is like unto the tongue of Ptah, my throat is even as that of Hathor, and I tell forth the words of my father Tmu with my lips. He it is who constrained the handmaid, the wife of Seb; and unto him are bowed [all] heads, and there is fear of him. Hymns of praise are sung in honour of my mighty deeds, and I am accounted the heir of Seb, the lord of the earth, the protector. The god Seb gives cool water, he makes his dawnings mine. They who dwell in Annu bow down their heads before me, for I am their bull. I grow strong from moment to moment; my loins are made strong for millions of years."

THE CHAPTER OF CHANGING INTO THE SOUL OF TMU

Says Osiris Ani, triumphant: "I have not entered into the house of destruction; I have not been brought to naught, I have not known decay. I am Ra who comes forth from Nu, the divine Soul, the creator of his own limbs. Sin is an abomination unto me, and I look not thereon; I cry not out against right and truth, but I have my being therein. I am the god Hu, and I never die in my name of 'Soul.' I have brought myself into being together with Nu in my name of 'Khepera.' In their forms have I come into being in the likeness of Ra. I am the lord of light."

THE CHAPTER OF CHANGING INTO A BENNU BIRD

Says Osiris, the scribe Ani, triumphant in peace:

"I came into being from unformed matter, I created myself in the image of the god Khepera, and I grew in the form of plants. I am hidden in the likeness of the Tortoise. I am formed out of the atoms of all the gods. I am the yesterday of the four [quarters of the world], and I am the seven uraei that came into existence in the East, the mighty one who illuminates the nations by his body. He is god in the likeness of Set; and Thoth dwells in the midst of them by judgement of the dweller in Sekhem and of the spirits of Annu. I sail among them, and I come; I am crowned, I am become a shining one, I am mighty, I am become holy among the gods. I am the god Khonsu who drives back all that opposes him."

THE CHAPTER OF CHANGING INTO A HERON

Says Osiris, the scribe Ani: "I have dominion over the beasts that are brought for sacrifice, with the knife held at their heads and their hair, for those who dwell in their emerald [fields], the ancient and the shining ones who make ready the hour of Osiris Ani, triumphant in peace. He makes slaughter upon earth, and I make slaughter upon earth. I am strong, and I have passed along the lofty path [that leads] unto heaven. I have made myself pure, with long strides I have gone unto my city, holding on my way to Sepu. I have established [the one who is] in Unnu. I have set the gods upon their places, and I have made glorious the temples of those who live in their shrines. I know the goddess Nut, I know the god Tatunen, I know Teshert, I have brought with me their horns. I know Heka, I have heard his words, I am the red calf that is drawn with the pen. When they hear [my words], the gods say: 'Let us bow down our faces, and let him come unto us; the light shines beyond you.' My hour is within my body. I have not spoken [evil] in the place of right and truth, and each day I advance in right and truth. I am shrouded in darkness when I sail up to celebrate the festival of the dead one, and to embalm the aged one, the guardian of the earth – I the Osiris, the scribe Ani, triumphant! I have not entered into the hiding places of the starry deities. I have ascribed glory unto Osiris. I have pacified the heart of the gods who follow after him. I have not felt fear of those who cause terror, even those who dwell in their own lands. Behold, I am exalted upon [my] resting place upon my throne. I am Nu, and I shall never be overthrown by the Evil-doer. I am the god Shu who sprang from unformed matter. My soul is god; my soul is eternity. I am the creator of darkness, and I appoint unto it a resting place in the uttermost parts of heaven. I am the prince of eternity, I am the exalted one [in] Nebu. I grow young in [my] city, I grow young in my homestead. My name is 'Never-failing.' My name is 'Soul, Creator of Nu, who makes his abode in the underworld.' My nest is not seen, and I have not broken my egg. I am lord of millions of years – I have made my nest in the uttermost parts of heaven. I have come down unto the earth of Seb. I have done away with my faults. I have seen my father as

This 19th Dynasty stele from Deir el Medina illustrates Thoth and the stars of Heaven.

the lord of Shautat. As concerning Osiris Ani, may his body dwell in Annu; may it be manifested unto those who are with the Shining One in the place of burial in Amenta…"

THE CHAPTER OF CHANGING INTO A LOTUS

Says Osiris Ani: "I am the pure lotus that comes forth from the god of light, the guardian of the nostrils of Ra, the guardian of the nose of Hathor. I advance and I hasten after him who is Horus. I am, the pure one who comes forth from the field."

THE CHAPTER OF CHANGING INTO THE GOD WHO GIVES LIGHT IN THE DARKNESS

Says Osiris, the scribe Ani, triumphant: "I am the girdle of the robe of the god Nu that shines and sheds light, that abides in his presence and sends forth light into the darkness, that knits together the two fighters who live in my body through the mighty spell of the words of my mouth, that raises up him that has fallen – for he who was with him in the valley of Abtu has fallen – and I rest. I have remembered him. I have carried away the god Hu from my city wherein I found him, and I have led away the darkness captive by my might. I have upheld the Eye [of the Sun] when its power waned at the coming of the festival of the fifteenth day, and I have weighed Sut in the heavenly mansions beside the aged one who is with him. I have endowed Thoth in the House of the Moon-god with all that is needful for the coming of the festival of the fifteenth day. I have carried off the urerit crown; right and truth are in my body. The months are of emerald and crystal. My homestead is among the sapphire furrows. I am the lady who sheds light in darkness. I have come to give forth light in darkness, and lo! it is lightened and made bright. I have illuminated the blackness and I have overthrown the destroyers. I have made obeisance unto those who are in darkness, and I have raised up those who wept and who had bidden their faces and had sunk down. Then did they look upon me. I am the Lady, and I will not let you hear concerning me."

THE CHAPTER OF NOT DYING A SECOND TIME

Says Osiris Ani, triumphant: "Hail, Thoth! What is it that has happened unto the holy children of Nut? They have done battle, they have upheld strife, they have done evil, they have created the fiends, they have made slaughter, they have caused trouble; in truth, in all their doings the mighty have worked against the weak. Grant, O might of Thoth, that which the god Tmu has decreed [may be done]! And thou regards not evil, nor art thou provoked to anger when they bring their years to confusion and throng in and push to disturb their months; for in all that they have done unto thee, they have worked iniquity in secret. I am thy writing palette, O Thoth, and I have brought unto thee thine ink jar. I am not of those who work iniquity in their secret places; let not evil happen unto me."

Says Osiris, the scribe Ani:

"Hail, Tmu! What manner [of land] is this into which I have come? It has not water, it has not air; it is deep unfathomable, it is black as the blackest night, and men wander helplessly therein. In it a man may

Stela of the Steward Mentuwoser (ca. 1944 BC). This rectangular stone stela honors an official named Mentuwoser. Clasping a piece of folded linen in his left hand, he sits at his funeral banquet, ensuring that he will always receive food offerings and that his family will honor and remember him forever. To the right of Mentuwoser, his son summons his spirit. His daughter holds a lotus, and his father offers a covered dish of food and a jug of beer.

This relief shows Cheti and his wife in front of a lavishly furnished offering table (Middle Kingdom, early 12th Dynasty).

not live in quietness of heart; nor may the longings of love be satisfied therein. But let the state of the Shining Ones be given unto me for water and for air and for the satisfying of the longings of love, and let quietness of heart be given unto me for bread and for ale. The god Tmu has decreed that I shall see his face, and that I shall not suffer from the things that pain him. May the gods hand on their thrones for millions of years. Thy throne has descended unto thy son Horus. The god Tmu has decreed that his course shall be among the holy princes.

In truth, he shall rule over thy throne, and he shall be heir to the throne of the dweller in the Lake of Fire. It has been decreed that in me he shall see his likeness, and that my face shall look upon the lord Tmu. How long then have I to live? It is decreed that thou shall live for millions of millions of years, a life of millions of years. May it be granted that I pass on unto the holy princes, for I am doing away with all that I did when this earth came into being from Nu, and when it sprang from the watery abyss even as it was in the days of old. I am Fate and Osiris and I have changed my form into the likeness of diverse serpents. Man knows not, and the gods cannot see, the two-fold beauty that I have made for Osiris, who is greater than all the gods. I have granted that he [shall rule] in the mount of the dead. Verily his son Horus is seated upon the throne of the dweller in the double Lake of Fire, as his heir. I have set his throne in the boat of millions of years. Horus is established upon his throne, amid the friends [of Osiris] and all that belonged unto him. Verily the soul of Sut, which is greater than all the gods, has departed to [Amenta]. May it be granted that I bind his soul in the divine boat at my will ... O my Osiris, thou has done for me that which thy father Ra did for thee. May I abide upon the earth lastingly; may I keep possession of my throne; may my heir be strong; may my tomb and my friends who are upon earth flourish; may my enemies be given over to destruction and to the shackles of the goddess Serq! I am thy son, and Ra is my father. For me likewise has thou made life, strength and health. Horus is established upon his throne. Grant that the days of my life may come unto worship and honour."

THE CHAPTER OF ENTERING INTO THE HALL OF DOUBLE RIGHT AND TRUTH: A HYMN OF PRAISE TO OSIRIS, THE DWELLER IN AMENTET

Osiris, the scribe Ani, triumphant, says: "I have come and I have drawn nigh to see thy beauties; my two hands are raised in adoration of thy name Right and Truth. I have drawn nigh unto the place where the acacia tree grows not, where the tree thick with leaves exists not, and where the ground yields neither herb nor grass. And I have entered into the place of secret and hidden things, I have conversed with the god Sut ... Osiris, the scribe Ani, has entered into the House of Osiris, and he has seen the hidden and secret things that are therein. The holy rulers of the pylons are in the form of shining ones. Anubis spoke unto him with the speech of man when he came from Ta-mera, saying, 'He knows our paths and our cities, I have been pacified, and the smell of him is to me even as the smell of one of you.'"

Ani says unto him: "I am Osiris, the scribe Ani, triumphant in peace, triumphant! I have drawn nigh to behold the great gods, and I feed upon the meals of sacrifice whereon their ka's feed. I have been to the boundaries [of the lands] of the Ram, the lord of Tattu, and he has granted that I may come forth as a bennu bird and that I may have the power of speech. I have passed through the river-flood. I have made offerings with incense. I have made my way by the side of the thick-leaved tree of the children. I have been in Abtu in the House of Satet. I have flooded and I have sunk the boat of my enemies. I have

Pharaoh makes an offering of a gold necklace, from the Mortuary Temple of Seti I at Abydos.

sailed forth upon the Lake in the neshem boat. I have seen the noble ones of Kam-ur. I have been in Tattu, and I have constrained myself to silence. I have set the divine form upon his two feet. I have been with the god Pa-tep-tu-f, and I have seen the dweller in the Holy Temple. I have entered into the House of Osiris, and I have arrayed myself in the apparel of him who is therein. I have entered into Re-stau, and I have beheld the hidden things that are therein. I have been swathed, but I found for myself a thoroughfare. I have entered into Anruft, and I have clothed my body with the apparel which is therein. The antu unguent of women has been given unto me … Verily, Sut spoke unto me the things that concern himself, and I said, 'I Let the thought of the trial of the balance by thee be even within our hearts.'"

The majesty of the god Anubis says: "Does thou know the name of this door to declare it unto me?" Osiris, the scribe Ani, triumphant, triumphant in peace, says: "'Driven away of Shu' is the name of this door." Says the majesty of the god Anubis: "Does thou know the name of the upper leaf and of the lower leaf thereof?" [Osiris, the scribe

Ani, triumphant in peace says]: "'Lord of right and truth, [standing] upon his two feet' is the name of the upper leaf, and 'Lord of might and power, dispenser of cattle' [is the name of the lower leaf]." [The majesty of the god Anubis says]: "Pass thou, for thou knows [the names], O Osiris, the scribe, teller of the divine offerings of all the gods of Thebes, Ani, triumphant, lord to be revered."

THE NEGATIVE CONFESSION

Ani says: "Hail, thou whose strides are long, who comes forth from Annu, I have not done iniquity."

"Hail, thou who art embraced by flame, who comes forth from Kheraba, I have not robbed with violence."

"Hail, Fentiu, who comes forth from Khemennu, I have not stolen."

"Hail, Devourer of the Shade, who comes forth from Qernet, I have done no murder; I have done no harm."

"Hail, Nehau, who comes forth from Re-stau, I have not defrauded offerings."

"Hail, god in the form of two lions, who comes forth from heaven, I have not diminished oblations."

"Hail, thou whose eyes are of fire, who comes forth from Saut, I have not plunderedthe god."

"Hail, thou Flame, which comes and goes, I have spoken no lies."

"Hail, Crusher of bones, who comes forth from Suten-henen, I have not snatched away food."

"Hail, thou who shoots forth the Flame, who comes forth from Het-Ptah-ka, I have not caused pain."

"Hail, Qerer, who comes forth from Amentet, I have not committed fornication."

"Hail, thou whose face is turned back, who comes forth from thy hiding place, I have not caused shedding of tears."

"Hail, Bast, who comes forth from the secret place, I have not dealt deceitfully."

"Hail, thou whose legs are of fire, who comes forth out of the darkness, I have not transgressed."

"Hail, Devourer of Blood, who comes forth from the block of slaughter, I have not acted guilefully."

"Hail, Devourer of the inward parts, who comes forth from Mabet, I have not laid waste the ploughed land."

"Hail, Lord of Right and Truth, who comes forth from the city of Right and Truth, I have not been an eavesdropper."

Stela of the family of Houyou, singer to the king. The centre panel shows Houyou making offerings to Osiris.

"Hail, thou who strides backwards, who comes forth from the city of Bast, I have not set my lips in motion [against any man]."

"Hail, Sertiu, who comes forth from Annu, I have not been angry and wrathful except for a just cause."

"Hail, thou being of two-fold wickedness, who comes forth from Ati I have not defiled the wife of any man."

"Hail, thou two-headed serpent, who comes forth from the torture chamber, I have not defiled the wife of any man."

"Hail, thou who regards what is brought unto thee, who comes forth from Pa-Amsu, I have not polluted myself."

"Hail, chief of the mighty, who comes forth from Amentet, I have not caused terror."

Offering drinks to the gods (Temple of Horus, Edfu).

"Hail, thou Destroyer, who comes forth from Kesiu, I have not transgressed."

"Hail, thou who orders speech, who comes forth from Urit, I have not burned with rage."

"Hail, thou Babe, who comes forth from Uab, I have not stopped my ears against the words of Right and Truth."

"Hail, Kenemti, who comes forth from Kenemet, I have not caused grief."

"Hail, thou who brings thy offering, I have not acted with insolence."

"Hail, thou who orders speech, who come forth from Unaset, I have not stirred up strife."

"Hail, Lord of faces, who comes forth from Netchfet, I have not judged hastily."

"Hail, Sekheriu, who comes forth from Utten, I have not been an eavesdropper."

"Hail, Lord of the two horns, who comes forth from Saïs, I have not multiplied words exceedingly."

"Hail, Nefer-Tmu, who comes forth from Het-Ptah-ka, I have done neither harm nor ill."

"Hail, Tmu in thine hour, who comes forth from Tattu, I have never cursed the king."

"Hail, thou who works with thy will, who comes forth from Tebu, I have never fouled the water.

"Hail, thou bearer of the sistrum, who comes forth from Nu, I have not spoken scornfully."

False door symbolising the gateway to the underworld, excavation site near the Pyramid of Teti, Saqqara (Sixth Dynasty, 24th–22nd century BC).

"Hail, thou who makes humankind flourish, who comes forth from Saïs, I have never cursed God."

"Hail, Nehebka, who comes forth from thy hiding place, I have not stolen."

"Hail, thou who sets in order the head, who comes forth from thy shrine, I have not plundered the offerings to the blessed dead."

"Hail, thou who brings thy arm, who comes forth from the city of Maati, I have not filched the food of the infant, neither have I sinned against the god of my native town."

"Hail, thou whose teeth are white, why comes forth from Ta-she, I have not slaughtered with evil intent the cattle of the god."

SCRIBE'S NOTE:

Osiris Ani, triumphant, is surrounded with [fine] raiment, he is shod with white sandals, and he is anointed with very precious anta ointment; and a bull, and herbs, and incense, and ducks, and flowers, and ale, and cakes have been offered unto him. And behold, thou shall draw upon a clean tile the image of a table of offerings in clean colours, and thou shall bury it in a field whereon swine have not trampled. If this word then be written upon it, he himself shall rise again (and his children's children shall flourish even as Ra flourishes without ceasing). He shall dwell in favour in the presence of the king among the chiefs, and cakes and cups of drink and portions of meat shall be given unto him upon the table of the great god. He shall not be thrust from any door in Amentet; he shall travel on together with the kings of the north and of the south, and he shall abide with the followers of Osiris near unto Unnefer, for ever, and for ever, and for ever.

THE CHAPTER OF A TET OF GOLD

Osiris Ani, triumphant, says: "Thou rises, O still heart! Thou shines, O still heart! Place thou thyself upon my side. I come, I bring unto thee a tet of gold; rejoice therein."

THE CHAPTER OF A BUCKLE OF CARNELIAN

Says Osiris Ani, triumphant: "The blood of Isis, the charms of Isis, the power of Isis, are a protection unto me, the chief, and they crush that which I abhor."

SCRIBE'S NOTE:

This chapter shall be said over a buckle of red carnelian (or jasper) that has been dipped in water of ankham flowers and inlaid in sycamore wood, and has been placed on the neck of the shining one. If this chapter be inscribed upon it, it shall become the power of Isis, and it shall protect him; and Horus, the son of Isis, shall rejoice when he sees it. No way shall be impassable to him, and one hand shall extend unto heaven, and the other unto earth. If this chapter be known [by the deceased] he shall be among those who

The architect Kha and his wife Merit worship Osiris, lord of the afterlife. From the Book of the Dead in the funerary chamber of Kha, 18th Dynasty (1540–1295 BC), Deir El-Medina.

follow Osiris Un-nefer, triumphant. The gates of the underworld shall be opened unto him, and a homestead shall be given unto him, together with wheat and barley, in the Sekhet-Aru; and the followers of Horus who reap therein shall proclaim his name as one of the gods who are therein.

Isis nursing Horus (ca. 1070–343 BC)

THE CHAPTER OF A HEART OF CARNELIAN

Says Osiris Ani, triumphant: "I am the bennu, the soul of Ra, and the guide of the gods into the underworld. The souls come forth upon earth to do the will of their ka's, and the soul of Osiris Ani comes forth to do the will of his ka."

THE CHAPTER OF THE PILLOW THAT IS PLACED UNDER THE HEAD OF OSIRIS ANI, TRIUMPHANT, TO WARD OFF WOES FROM THE DEAD BODY OF OSIRIS

[Ani says]: "Lift up thy head to the heavens, for I have knit thee together triumphantly. Ptah has overthrown his foes and thine; all his enemies have fallen, and they shall never more rise up again, O Osiris."

DIVINE UTTERANCES

[Isis says:] "I have come to be a protector unto thee. I waft unto thee air for thy nostrils, and the north wind, which comes forth from the god Tmu, unto thy nose – I have made whole thy lungs. I have made thee to be like unto a god. Thine enemies have fallen beneath thy feet. Thou has been made victorious in Nut, and thou art mighty to prevail with the gods."

[Nephthys says:] "I have gone round about to protect thee, brother Osiris; I have come to be a protector unto thee. [My strength shall be behind thee, my strength shall be behind thee, for ever. Ra has heard thy cry, and the gods have granted that thou should be victorious. Thou art raised up, and thou art victorious over that which has been done unto thee. Ptah has thrown down thy foes, and thou art Horus, the son of Hathor.]"

[The flame of Isis says:] "I protect thee with this flame, and I drive away him (the foe) from the valley of the tomb, and I drive away the sand from thy feet. I embrace Osiris Ani, who is triumphant in peace and in right and truth."

[The flame of Nephthys says:] "I have come to hew in pieces. I am not hewn in pieces, nor will I suffer thee to be hewn in pieces. I have come to do violence, but I will not let violence be done unto thee, for I am protecting thee."

[The Tet says:] "I have come quickly, and I have driven back the footsteps of the god whose face is hidden. I have illuminated his sanctuary. I stand behind the sacred Tet or, the day of repulsing disaster. I protect thee, O Osiris."

[Mestha says:] I am Mestha, thy son, O Osiris Ani, triumphant. I have come to protect thee, and I will make thine abode flourish everlastingly.

I have commanded Ptah, even as Ra himself commanded him."

[Hapi says:] "I am Hapi thy son, O Osiris Ani, triumphant. I have come to protect thee. Thy head and thy limbs are knit together; and I have smitten down thine enemies beneath thee. I have given unto thee thy head for ever and for ever, O Osiris Ani, triumphant in peace."

Stela of Pekysis (1st century BC–4th century AD). Flanked by Anubis and Osiris are Pekysis, son of Aruotes, his brother Pachoumis, Tbaikis the elder and Tbaikis the younger.

[Tuamautef says:] "I am thy beloved son Horus. I have come to avenge thee, O my father Osiris, upon him that did evil unto thee; and I have put him under thy feet for ever, and for ever, and for ever; O Osiris Ani, triumphant in peace."

[Qebhsennuf says:] "I am thy son, O Osiris Ani, triumphant. I have come to protect thee. I have collected thy bones, and I have gathered together thy members. [I have brought thy heart and I have placed it upon its throne within thy body. I have made thy house to flourish after thee, O thou who lives for ever.]"

[The bird that faces the setting sun says]: "Praise be to Ra when he sets in the western part of heaven. Osiris Ani, triumphant in peace in the underworld, says: 'I am a perfected soul.'"

[The bird that faces the rising sun says]: "Praise be to Ra when he rises in the eastern part of heaven from Osiris Ani, triumphant."

[The Perfected Soul says]: "I am a perfected soul in the holy egg of the abtu fish. I am the great cat that dwells in the seat of right and truth wherein rises the god Shu."

[The text near the ushabti figure reads]: Osiris Ani, the overseer, triumphant, says: " Hail, ushabti figure! If it be decreed that Osiris [Ani] shall do any of the work that is to be done in the underworld, let all that stands in the way be removed from before him; whether it be to plough the fields, or to fill the channels with water, or to carry sand from [the East to the West]." The ushabti figure replies: "I will do [it]; verily I am here [when] thou calls."

HERE BEGIN THE CHAPTERS OF THE SEKHET-HETEPU AND THE CHAPTERS OF COMING FORTH BY DAY, AND OF GOING INTO AND OF COMING OUT FROM THE UNDERWORLD, AND OF ARRIVING IN THE SEKHET-ARU, AND OF BEING IN PEACE IN THE GREAT CITY WHEREIN ARE FRESH BREEZES.

Let me have power there. Let me become strong to plough there. Let me reap there. Let me eat there. Let me drink there. [Let me woo there.] And let me do all these things there, even as they are done upon earth.

Stela of Nakht (ca. 1950–1900 BC)

Says Osiris Ani, triumphant: "Set has carried away Horus to see what is being built in the Field of Peace, and he spreads the air over the divine soul within the egg in its day. He has delivered the innermost part of the body of Horus from the holy ones of Aker. Behold I have sailed in the mighty boat on the Lake of Peace. I, even I, have crowned him in the House of Shu. His starry abode renews its youth, renews its youth. I have sailed on its Lake that I may come unto its cities, and I have drawn nigh It unto the city Hetep. For behold, I repose at the seasons [of Horus]. I have passed through the region of the company of the gods who are aged and venerable. I have pacified the two holy Fighters who keep ward upon life. I have done that which is right and fair, and I have brought an offering and have pacified the two holy Fighters. I have cut off the hairy scalps of their adversaries, and I have made ended the woes that befell [their] children; I have done away all the evil that came against their souls; I have dominion over it, I have knowledge thereof. I have sailed forth on the waters [of the lake] that I may come unto the cities thereof. I have power over my mouth, being furnished [with]

Ani and his wife Tutu before a table of offerings.

charms; let not [the fiends] get the mastery over me, let them not have dominion over me. May I be equipped in thy Fields of Peace. What thou wishes, thou shall do [says the god]."

ANI BEFORE RA

Says Osiris Ani, triumphant: "Homage to thee, O thou lord, thou lord of right and truth, the One, the lord of eternity and creator of everlastingness, I have come unto thee, O my lord Ra. I have made

Hathor, goddess of the sky, of women, and of fertility and love.

meat offerings unto the seven kine (cows) and unto their bull. O ye who give cakes and ale to the shining ones, grant ye to my soul to be with you. May Osiris Ani, triumphant, be born upon your thighs; may he be like unto one of you for ever and for ever; and may he become a glorious being in the beautiful Amenta."

ADDRESS TO THE RUDDERS

"Hail, thou beautiful Power, beautiful rudder of the northern heaven."

"Hail, thou who goes round about heaven, thou pilot of the world, thou beautiful rudder of the western heaven."

"Hail, thou shining one, who lives in the temple wherein are the gods in visible forms, thou beautiful rudder of the eastern heaven."

"Hail, thou who dwells in the temple of the bright-faced ones, thou beautiful rudder of the southern heaven."

ADDRESS TO THE FOUR TRIADS

"Hail, ye gods who are above the earth, ye pilots of the underworld."

"Hail, ye mother gods who are above the earth, who are in the underworld, and who are in the House of Osiris."

"Hail, ye gods, ye pilots of Tasert, ye who are above the earth, ye pilots of the underworld."

"Hail, ye followers of Ra, who are in the train of Osiris."

A HYMN OF PRAISE TO OSIRIS THE DWELLER IN AMENTET, UN-NEFER WITHIN ABTU

Osiris Ani, triumphant, says: "Hail, O my lord, who traverses eternity, and whose existence endures for ever. Hail, Lord of Lords, King of Kings, Prince, the God of gods who live with Thee, I have come unto Thee. Make thou for me a seat with those who are in the underworld, and who adore the images of thy ka and who are among those who [endure] for millions of millions of years… May no delay arise for me in Ta-mera. Grant thou that they all may come unto me, great as well as small. May thou grant unto the ka of Osiris Ani [the power] to go into and to come forth from the underworld; and suffer him not to be driven back at the gates of the Tuat."

TO HATHOR

Hathor, lady of Amentet, dweller in the land of Urt, lady of Ta-sert, the Eye of Ra, the dweller in his brow, the beautiful Face in the Boat of Millions of Years… [a few undecipherable words follow].

GLOSSARY

The terms and names used in *The Egyptian Book of the Dead* were accumulated over many centuries and many may not have been fully understood by the ancient Egyptians themselves – hence the need for scribes to add notes here and there to try to explain the meaning.

In addition, the Egyptians often used metaphor in their writing and this can make it difficult for us to understand exactly what is being said. One of the most arresting terms used in the text, for example, is 'The Great Cackler', which refers to the primeval god of the earth, Geb, who was thought to have taken the form of a goose and produced an egg from which the sun god Ra emerged at the beginning of the world.

Names of demons are sprinkled throughout the text because it was believed that knowing the name of the demon or minor god gave the deceased power over it. What was important was knowing the name, not necessarily the meaning of that name. Some relevant examples include: 'The Eyeless One', 'He Who Lives On Maggots', 'She of the Knife', and 'Scowler'.

Our modern appreciation of the text is further complicated by the fact that sometimes we simply do not know what the ancient Egyptian word means. These words are indicated in the text by the appearance of the word in italics. Similarly, although we know where many of the cities and towns mentioned in the text were, there are many that remain a mystery.

Finally, for further reference, the name now usually applied to some of Wallis Budge's translations is given in brackets below.

Abtu. A sacred Nile fish associated with Abydos (also used for Abydos).

Abydos. One of the oldest cities in ancient Egypt and burial place of the early kings. It was later venerated as the burial place of the god Osiris.

Akert. 'The Silent Land' of the dead.

Amemet (Ammit). A monster present at the weighing of the heart who was ready to eat the heart if the judgement went against the deceased.

Amenta. 'The West', in the sense of 'where the sun sets'). The land of the dead.

Amentet. Goddess and personification of the 'Land of the West' or other world.

Amsu. A manifestation of the god Horus (see Horus).

'Ancient One'. A title of the sun god Ra who emerged at the creation of the world.

Anmutef (Iunmutef). A priestly god of the dead who looks after the deceased as a father looks after a child.

Anubis. A jackal-headed god associated with mummification and the afterlife. He is sometimes considered to be a son of the god Osiris.

Annu (Iunu). An ancient city later known as Heliopolis. The centre of worship of the god Ra.

Anreti (Anjety). The city later known as Busiris in the Nile delta.

Anrutf. 'The sterile'. A mystical region of the Other World.

Apep. A serpent demon with whom the sun-god Ra battled each night.

Apuat (Wepwawet). The 'Opener of the Way'. A wolf-god associated with Osiris.

Arit. A gate in the Other World – one of seven through which the deceased must pass.

Aru (Sekhet-Aru). The 'Field of Reeds'. An idealized version of the deceased's earthly life.

Ass. As in 'I smite the Ass'. A reference to the god of chaos Seth who murdered his brother Osiris.

Astes (Astennu). One of the baboons associated with the god of wisdom Thoth.

Atum. An ancient creator god associated with the city of Annu (Iunu).

***Bennu* bird.** A bird-god associated with the sun, creation, and rebirth. The bennu bird may have inspired the concept of a phoenix.

Bight of the Fiery Lake. Bay on the shore of the 'Lake of Fire' in which the wicked are punished.

Bull. A manifestation of Osiris.

'Coming forth'. The rising of the parts of the soul of the deceased.

Disc. The visible disc of the sun worshipped independently as the Aten.

Double lion. The primeval earth god Aker (Naker).

Egg of the Great Cackler. The egg produced by the primeval god Geb in the form of a goose from which the sun god Ra emerged.

Fields of Aru. The Field of Reeds. An idealized version of the deceased's earthly life.

Geb (the Erpat). A primeval god personifying the earth and the father of Osiris.

Great Balance. The set of scales used at the judgment of the deceased. The heart of the deceased was weighed against the feather of maat (cosmic order/'right'). In order to pass the judgement the heart must weigh the same.

Great Cackler. The primeval god Geb manifested as a goose who produced an egg from which emerged the sun god Ra.

Hall of Osiris/of Double Truth. The great hall in which Osiris oversees the judgement of the deceased and in which the tribunal of gods sits.

Hapi. The god of the Nile.
Also the name of one of the sons of Horus.

Hathor. An ancient goddess of femininity who was also ``mistress of the West' and welcomed the deceased to the Afterlife.

Heka. A god who personified medicine and magic.

Horus. An ancient, multi-faceted, and complex falcon god. The son of Osiris and Isis who sought to avenge the murder of his father by his uncle Seth.

Hu. The divine personification of the first word uttered at the creation of the world by the god Atum.

Isis. A protective goddess of life and magic. Wife of Osiris and mother of Horus.

ka. An element of the individual spirit or 'soul' of the deceased released upon death.

Khemennu. The city of Hermopolis on the boundary of Upper and Lower Egypt.

Khent-en-maa (Khenti-Amentiu). A jackal-headed god whose name was also used as a title for Osiris and Anubis The name means 'Foremost of the Westerners' (that is, the dead).

Khepera (Khepri). Deity of the young sun represented as a scarab beetle.

Kheraba. A city on the east bank of the Nile close to Hermopolis.

Khu (akh). Part of the spirit or 'soul' of the deceased represented by light, into which the deceased was transfigured.

Lake of Fire. A place of punishment of the wicked in the Other World.

Lake of Peace. A lake within the Other World that must be crossed by ferry in order to reach the Field of Reeds.

Leg of the Sky. Ursa Major or the Plough.

Lion-god. The lion-headed god Maahes. He promoted order and justice by punishing those who transgressed against cosmic order (see maat).

Maat. A goddess personifying justice, truth

and cosmic order and recognizable by the ostrich feather she wear on her head. It was against this feather that the heart of the deceased was weighed during the judgment.

Maat. The ancient Egyptian concept of truth, justice and cosmic order which all Egyptians were expected to abide by in life.

Maau (mau). The Egyptian cat and a manifestation of the sun god Ra, among other deities. The mau is possibly the ancestor of all domestic cats.

Manu. 'The land of Manu' means the west where the sun god Ra set each day. The abode of the dead to the west of the river Nile.

Mehurt (Mehet-Weret). An ancient cow goddess who gave birth to the sun god Ra in one version of the ancient Egyptian creation myths.

Memphis. Inebu-hedj, the ancient capital of Egypt.

Menhu (Min). An Upper Egyptian god of fertility.

Mesqet. The eastern region where the sun rises.

Naarutef. A region of the Other World meaning 'it never sprouts'.

Naker (Aker). A primeval double-lion earth god. The boat of Ra travels over the back of Aker in the Other World.

Neb-er-tcher. A manifestation of Osiris.

Nekhbet. The vulture goddess protector of Upper Egypt.

Nekhen. A city and cult centre of the god Horus in Upper Egypt.

Nephthys. The protective goddess sister of Isis, Osiris, and Seth. The mother of Anubis.

Neter-khert. The abode of the dead.

Nu (Nun). The personification of the primeval waters from which creation emerged.

Nut. The goddess of the sky and mother of Isis, Nephthys, Osiris and Seth.

Osiris Un-nefer (Wennefer). A manifestation of Osiris as the judge of the dead.

Pe. Together with Dep (Tep), Pe formed the city of Buto in the Nile Delta where the patron goddess of Lower Egypt, Wadjet, had her temple and oracle.

***Persea* tree.** The sacred tree of ancient Egypt which, perhaps, originated in a religious context in Heliopolis (associated with the sun-god Ra). The leaves and fruits were used in funerals.

Pool of Fire (Lake of Fire). A place of punishment of the wicked in the Other World.

Ptah/Ptah-Seker-Tem (Ptah-Seker-Tatenen). Ptah was the creator god of Memphis. Ptah-Seker-Tatenen (or -Osiris) was a hybrid god associated with the Other World.

Punt. An ancient and exotic trading partner probably located in the area of the Horn of Africa.

Qebhsennuf (Qebehsenuef). One of the sons of Horus.

Qernet. The region between Aswan and Philae.

Ra. The ancient sun god whose centre of worship was at Heliopolis (Iunu/Annu). Ra created all living things.

Ram. A manifestation of the god Osiris.

Re-stau. The passage that leads from the tomb to the Other World.

Sa (Sia). A divine manifestation of perception who travelled with, and helped, Ra on his night time journey through the Other World.

Sah. The (male) divine personification of the constellation of Orion.

Saïs. A town in the western Nile delta.

Sameref. A priestly god who represented the deceased during the judgement before Osiris.

Satet (Satis). A protective goddess of the border between Egypt and Nubia and associated with Elephantine Island (Aswan).

Sebek (Sobek). A crocodile-headed god of (among other things) power, fertility and protection.

Seker (Sokar). A falcon-headed god of the dead associated with Memphis.

Sekhet-Aru. The 'Field of Reeds'. An idealised form of the deceased's life on earth.

Sekhet-hetepet. 'The Field of Offerings' – another description of the 'Field of Reeds'. The idealised form of the deceased's mortal life within the kingdom of Osiris.

Sekhem. Principally a sceptre of power associated with Osiris who was referred to as the 'Great Sekhem'.

Sektet (mesektet) boat. The solar boat on which travelled through the Other World at night.

Sepa. A protective centipede god associated with Osiris and Horus.

Sept (Sopdet). The (female) divine personification of the star Sirius associated with Osiris.

Serq (Serket). A protective scorpion goddess of medicine, magic and healing of stings and bites.

Seshet. The goddess of wisdom, knowledge, and writing who is associated with architecture, building, mathematics. She helps the deceased transition to the Other World.

Set-Amentet (Amentet). The divine personification of the 'west' (the place were the sun sets) and where the sun sets), symbolic of death.

Shenit. The tribunal of 42 gods who the deceased to whom the deceased makes confesses.

Shining Ones. The 'Seven Shining Ones' were the protectors of Osiris and included the four sons of Horus.
Shu. A primeval god of peace, the air and the wind. The grandfather of Osiris, Isis, Nephthys, and Seth (Sut).

Smam-ur. The spirit of the primeval god Geb.

Smu metal. Probably electrum, a gold-silver alloy.

Suten-Henen (Henen-Nesut). A city in Lower Egypt later called Heracleopolis Magna.

Suti. The god Seth (see Sut).

Sut (Set; Seth). The son of Geb and Nut. The murderer of his brother Osiris.

Tanenet. A location sacred to Osiris and Ptah near Memphis.

Ta-sert. A name for the tomb.

Ta-she. The Fayum oasis, the 'Land of the Lakes'.

Tattu (Tettet). The city of Busiris in the Nile delta.

Tefnut. The goddess of moisture, dew and rain. The sister of Shu and the mother of Geb and Nut. Grandmother of Osiris.

Tep (Dep). Together with Pe, Dep formed the city of Buto in the Nile delta.

Tet (of gold). A measure of weight.

Tchafi. 'The two fledglings'. Manifestations of the god Horus—Horus the Protector of his father (Osiris) and Horus the Eyeless.

Tchatcha. The tribunal at the judgement of the deceased.

Tmu (Atum). A creation god who constitutes the physical presence of the world and universe. All things are made from his flesh.

Tmu-Heru-Khuti (Harmachis; Horemakhet). A manifestation of Horus as the rising sun.

Tuat (Duat). The Other World or realm of the dead through which the sun-god Ra travels each night and where Osiris, Anubis, Thoth, Hathor, Horus, and Maat appear to the deceased.

Thoth. The ibis-headed god of writing and magic who traveled with the sun-god Ra. He was the recorder of the judgement of the dead.

'Two Fighters'. Horus and Seth/Sut. Horus the son of Osiris and his uncle Seth (who had murdered his brother Osiris) locked in combat.

Tuamautef (Duamutef). One of the sons of Horus.

Uatchit (Wadjet). The cobra goddess protector of Lower Egypt and, later, together with Nekhbet, of all Egypt.

Unnu (Iunu). Heliopolis, the centre of worship of the sun-god Ra.

Uraeus (plural uraei). The rearing cobra symbol of the goddess Wadjet associated with royalty and gods.

Ushabti (shabti). Small figurines placed in a tomb. In the afterlife they would act as servants that would undertake manual work on behalf of the deceased.

Utchat (wedjat). The 'Eye of Horus'. A powerful and ubiquitous symbol of protection based on the eye of a falcon.

Picture credits

Alamy: 15 (Werner Forman/Musees Royaux du Cinquantenaire/Heritage Images), 21 (BasPhoto), 28 (Magica), 35 (Prisma Archivo), 36 (Peter Horree), 42 (Ian Dagnall Computing), 45 (Alain Guilleux), 50 (Interfoto), 57 (Agefotostock), 62 (Granger Historical Picture Archive), 66 (Science History Images), 78 & 83 (Chronicle), 86 (Prisma Archivo), 91 (Heritage Image Partnership), 108 (funkyfood London - Paul Williams), 114 (World History Archive), 117 (Heritage Image Partnership), 121 (BibleLandPictures), 123 (The Print Collector), 132 (BasPhoto), 137 (funkyfood London - Paul Williams), 139 (Peter Horree), 141 (Prisma Archivo), 145 (Granger Historical Picture Archive), 150 (Imagedoc), 165 (Peter Horree), 175 (Magica), 181 & 186 (Peter Horree), 190 (Prisma Archivo), 196 (Peter Horree), 197 (Jon Bower Egypt), 215 (Chronicle), 216 (vkstudio)

Getty Images: 13 (Fine Art), 41 (Art Media/Print Collector), 53 (Werner Forman), 58 & 77 (CM Dixon/Print Collector), 92 & 98 (Heritage Images), 110 (De Agostini), 118 (Photo12/Universal Images Group), 125 (duncan1890), 126, 131 & 149 (CM Dixon/Print Collector), 153 (Universal Images Group), 158 (Heritage Images), 162 (De Agostini), 166 (Luis Dafos), 172 (Sherri Damlo, Damlo Shots), 201 (De Agostini/S Vannini), 205 (Leemage)

Metropolitan Museum of Art, New York: 19, 25, 27, 49, 54, 61, 69, 70, 73, 88, 101, 102, 113, 157, 171, 176, 185, 206, 210, 213

Public Domain: 107

Line illustrations by Nadii Oborska, Sidhe and Tan_tan all via Shutterstock